CHINCHILLA COLORING BOOK

CRYSTAL
COLORING BOOKS

ISBN-13: 978-1979701570
ISBN-10: 1979701571

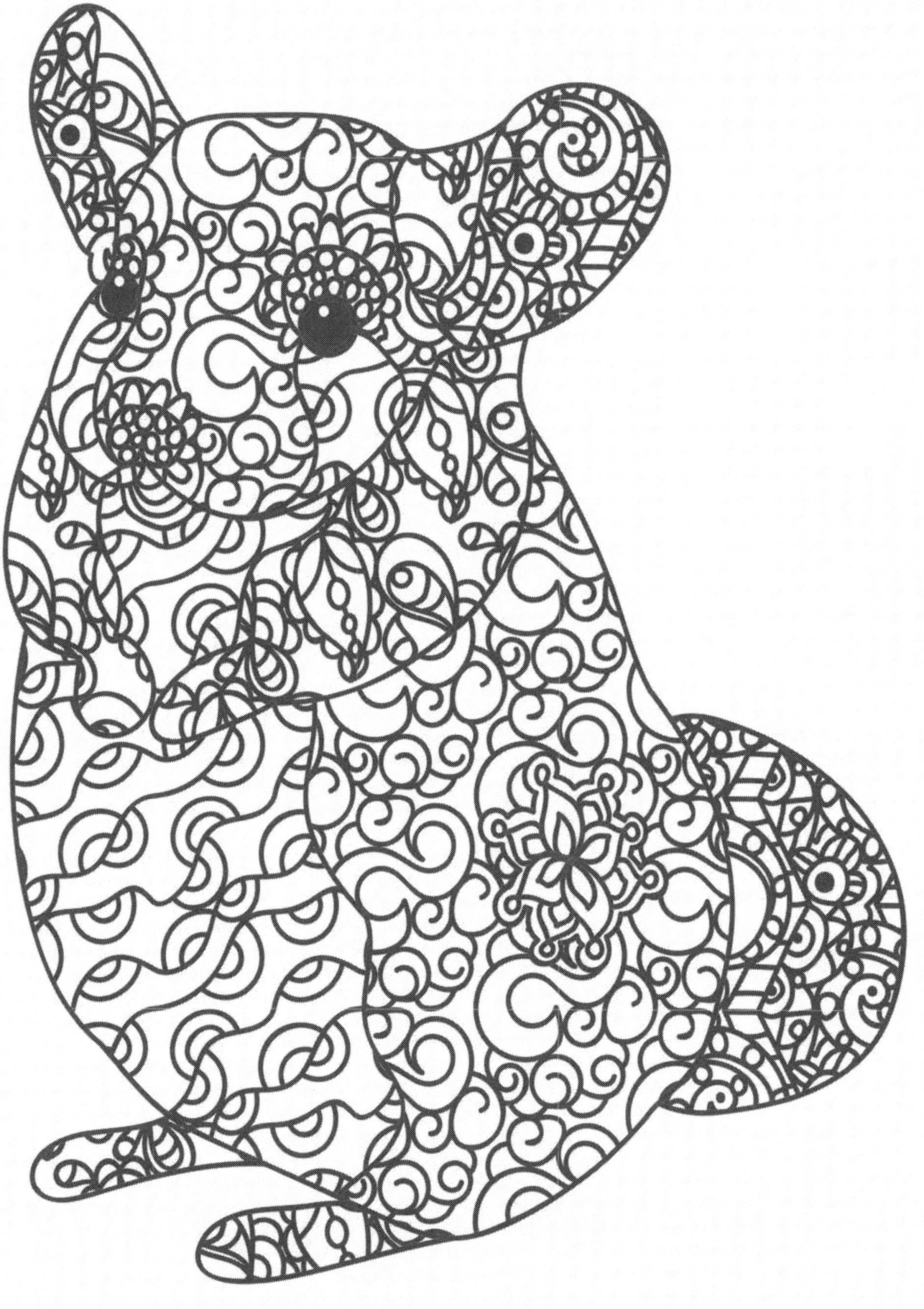

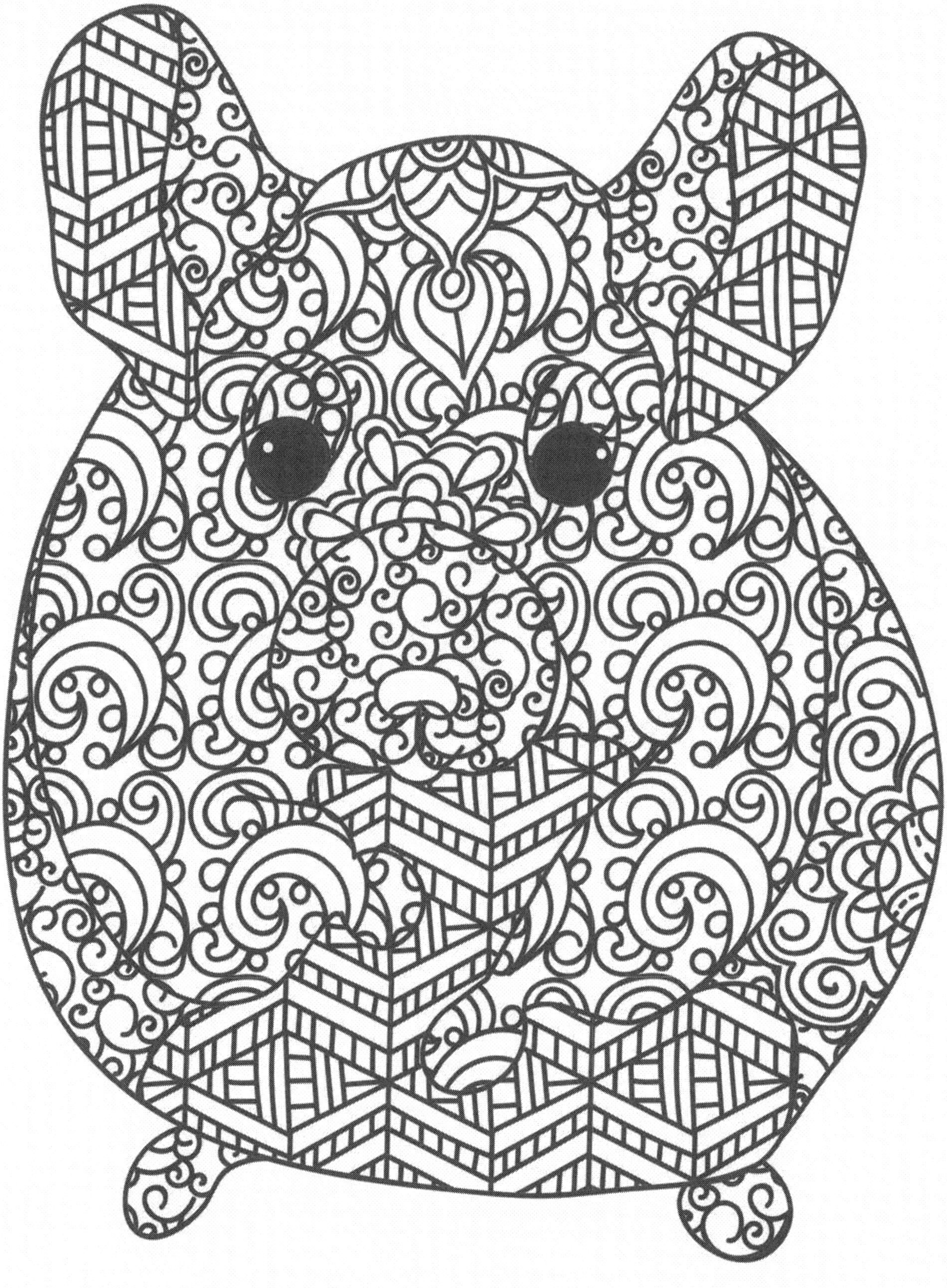

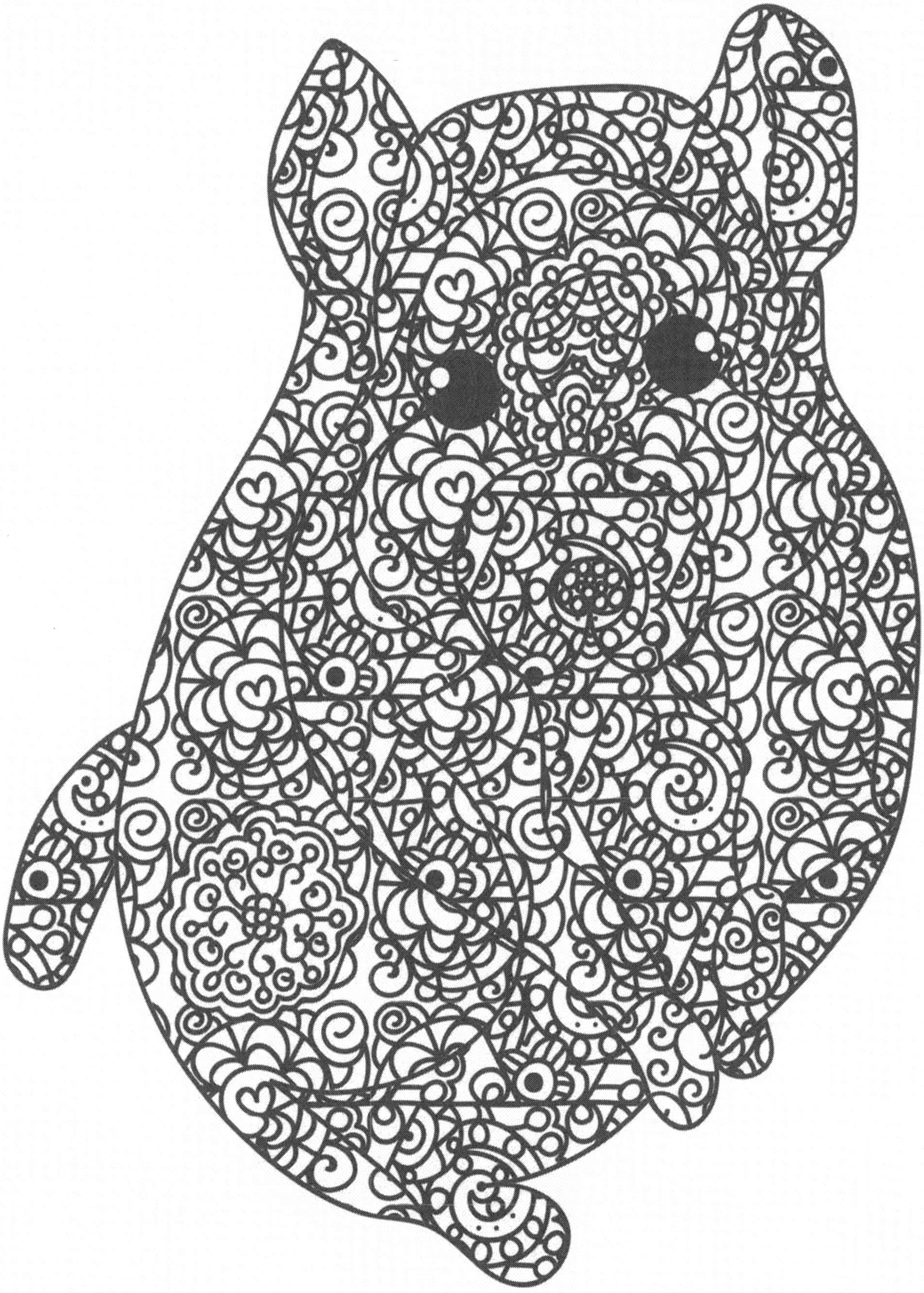

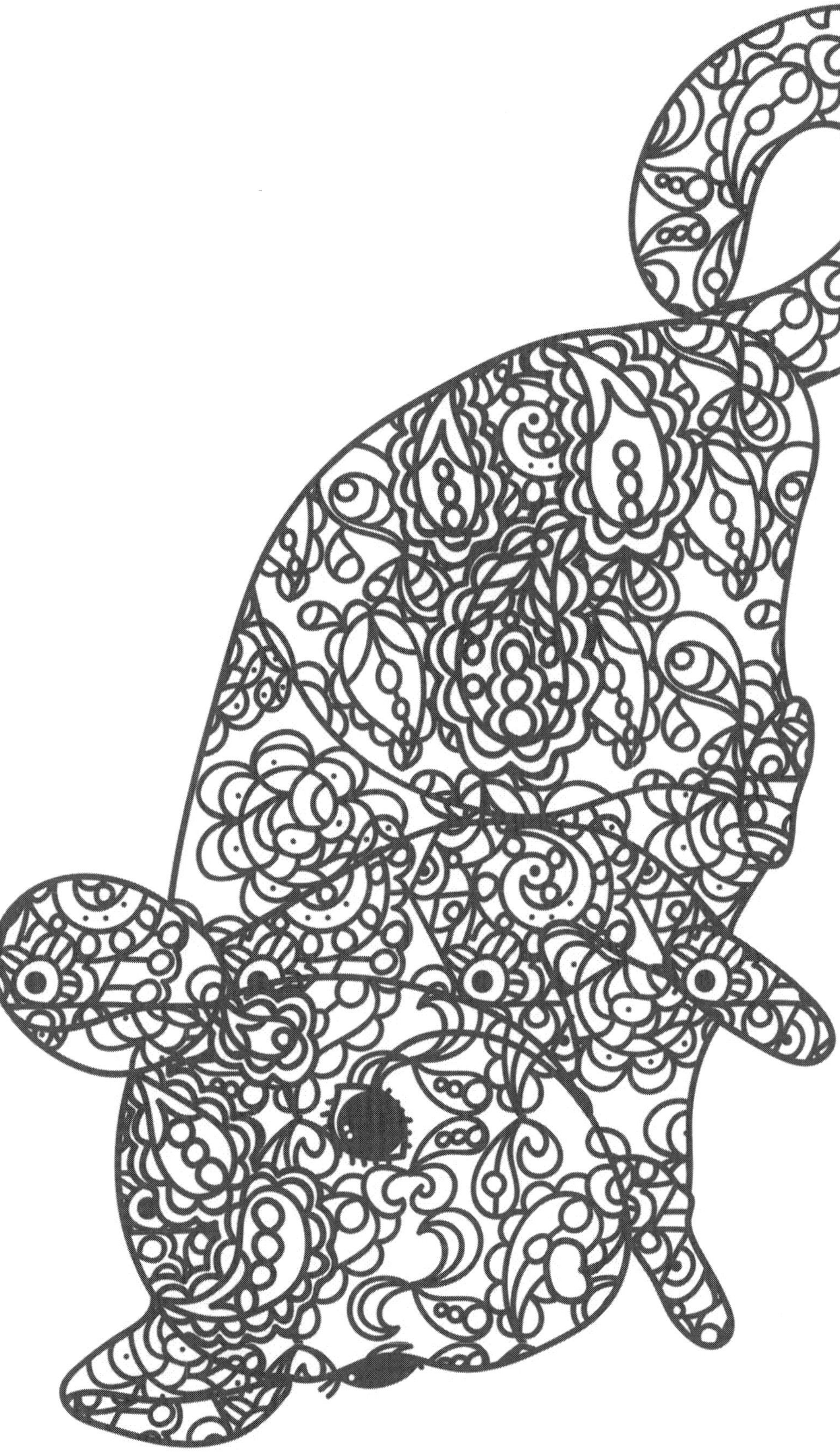

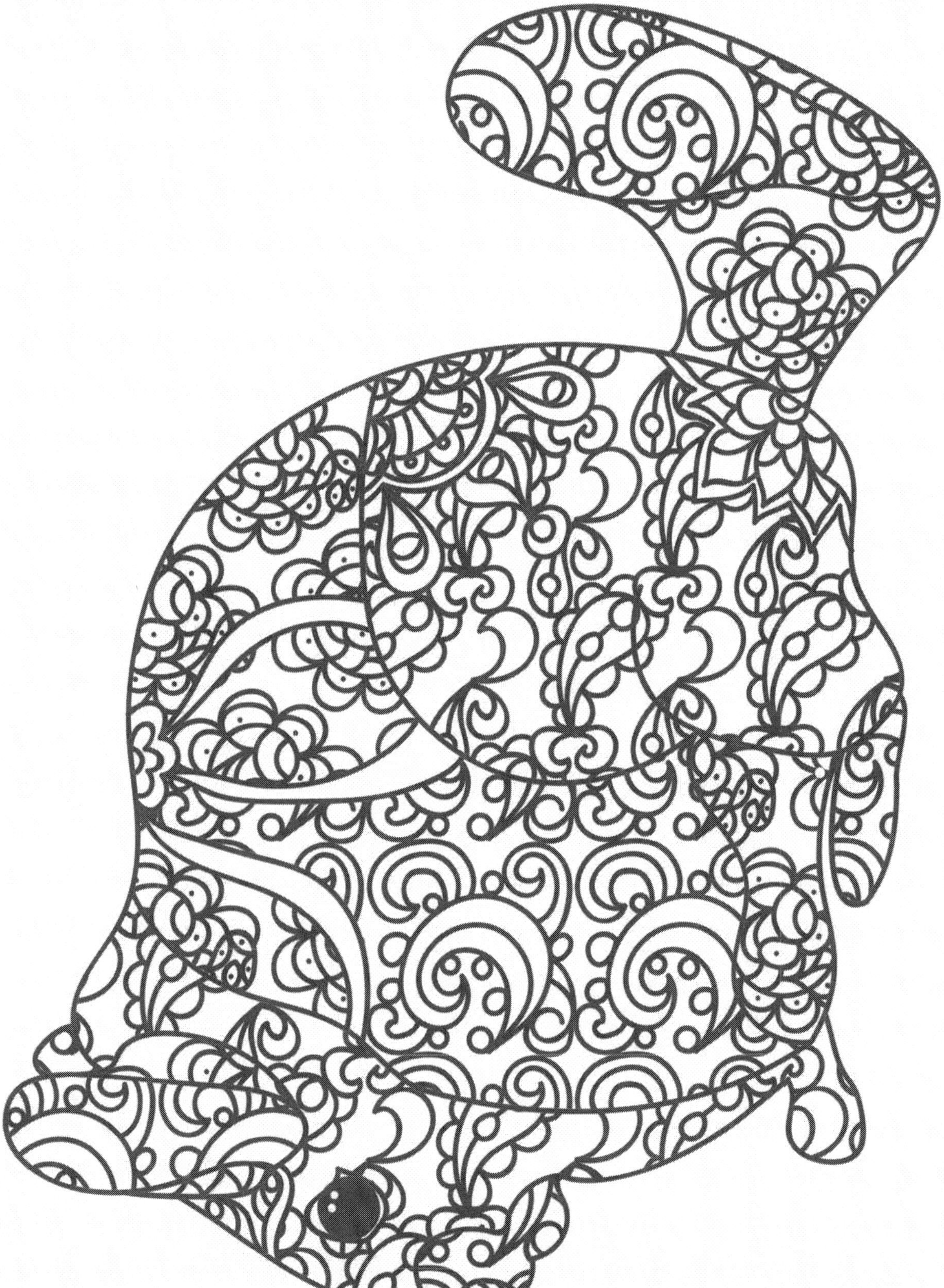

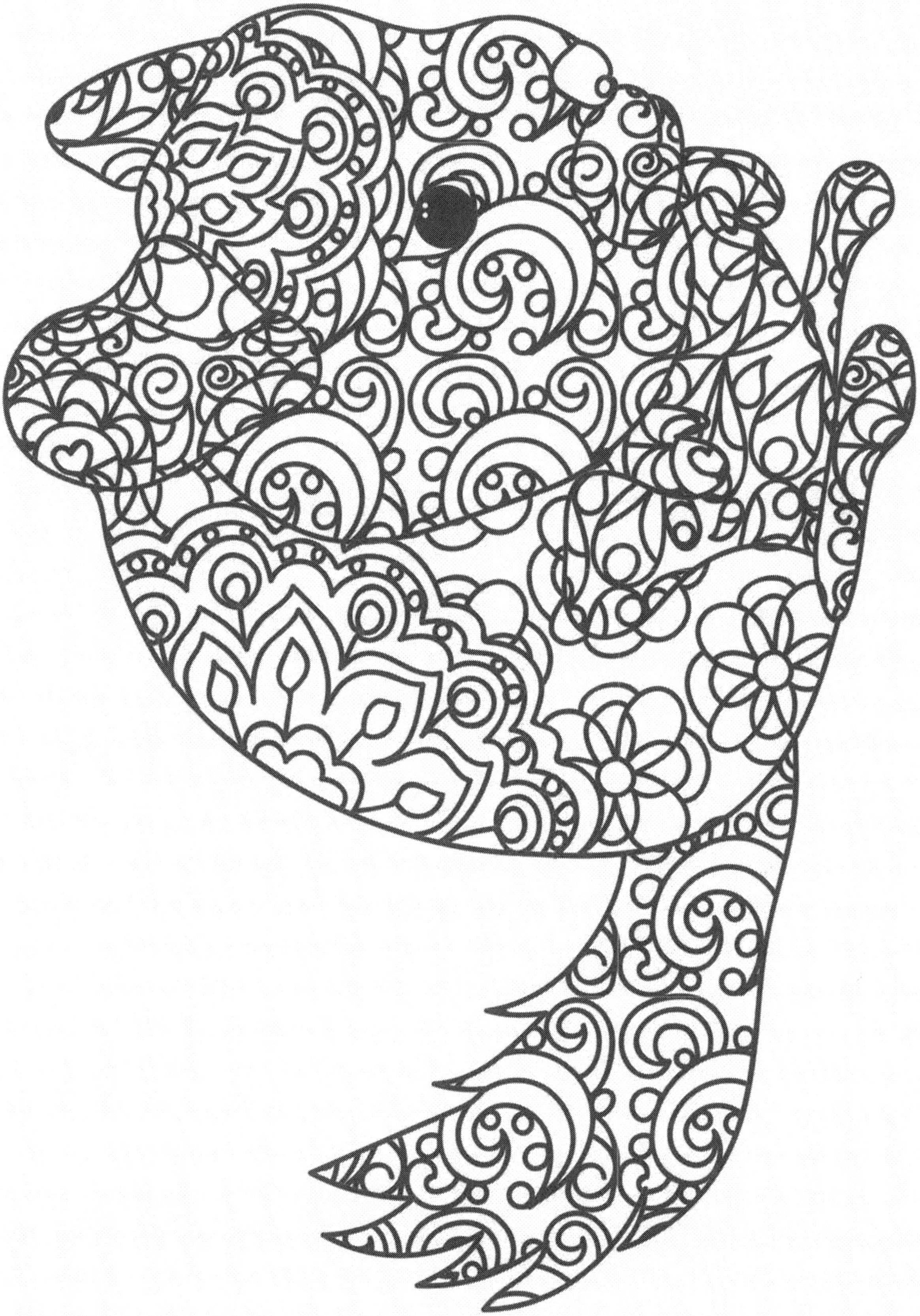

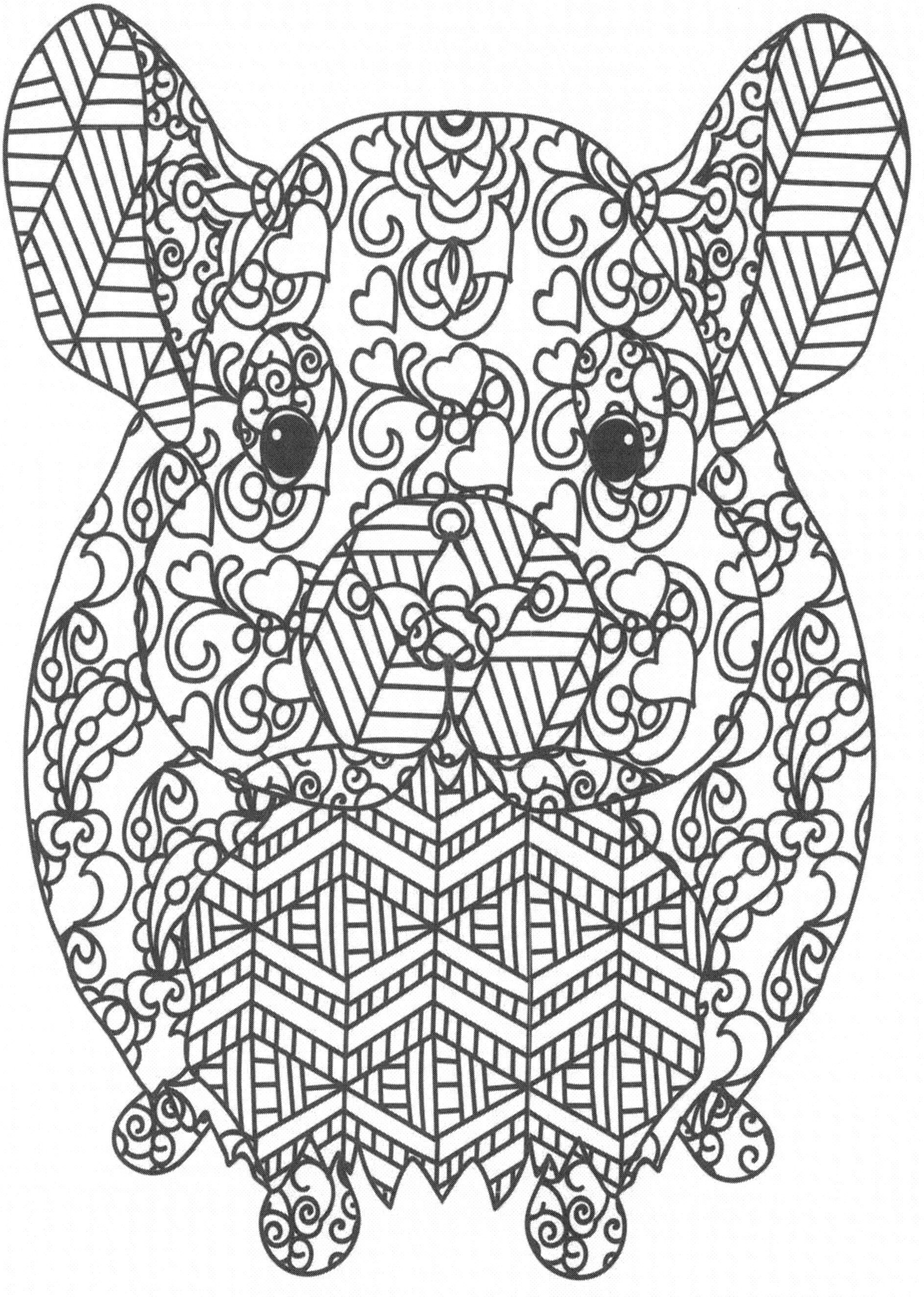

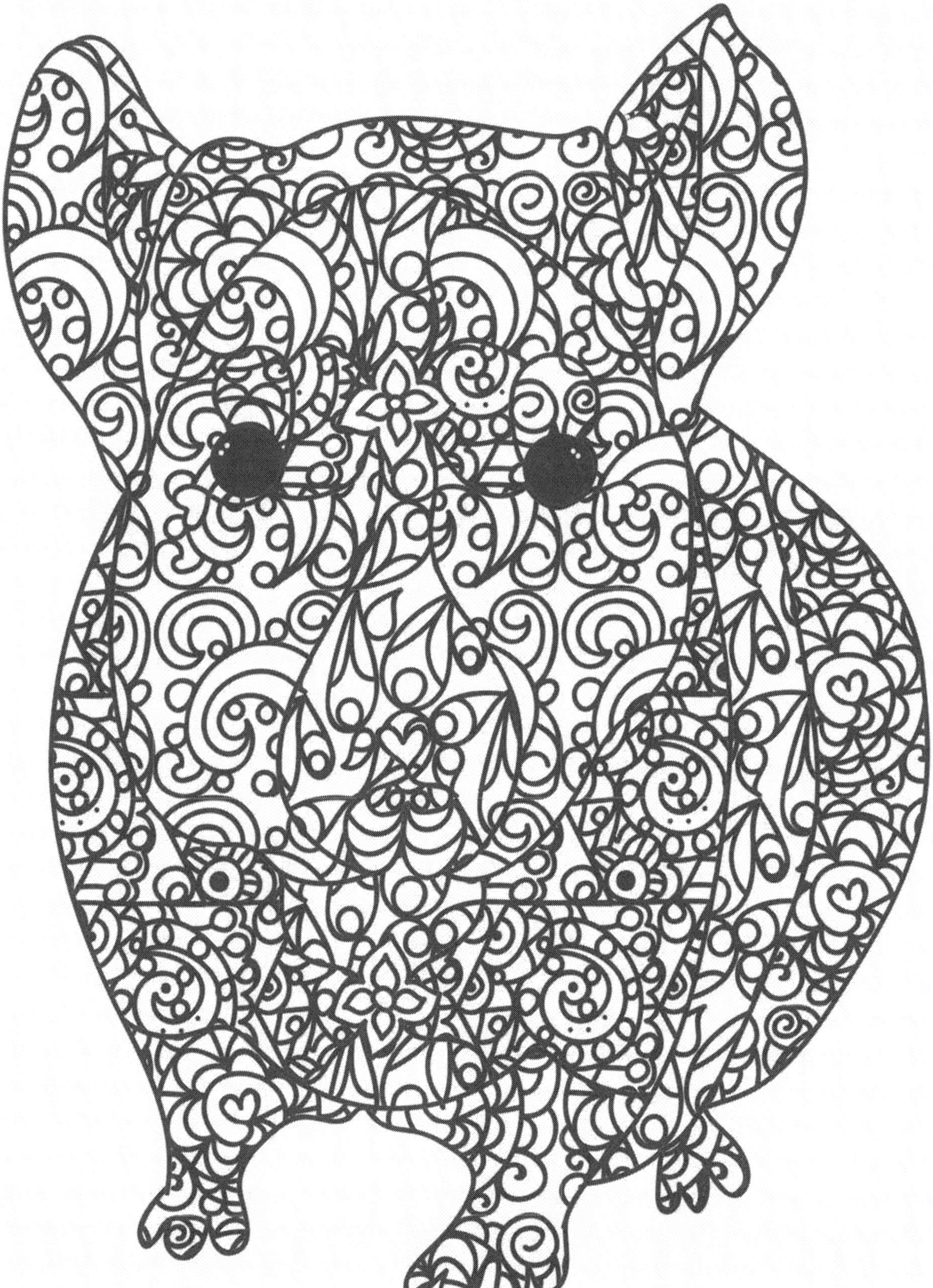

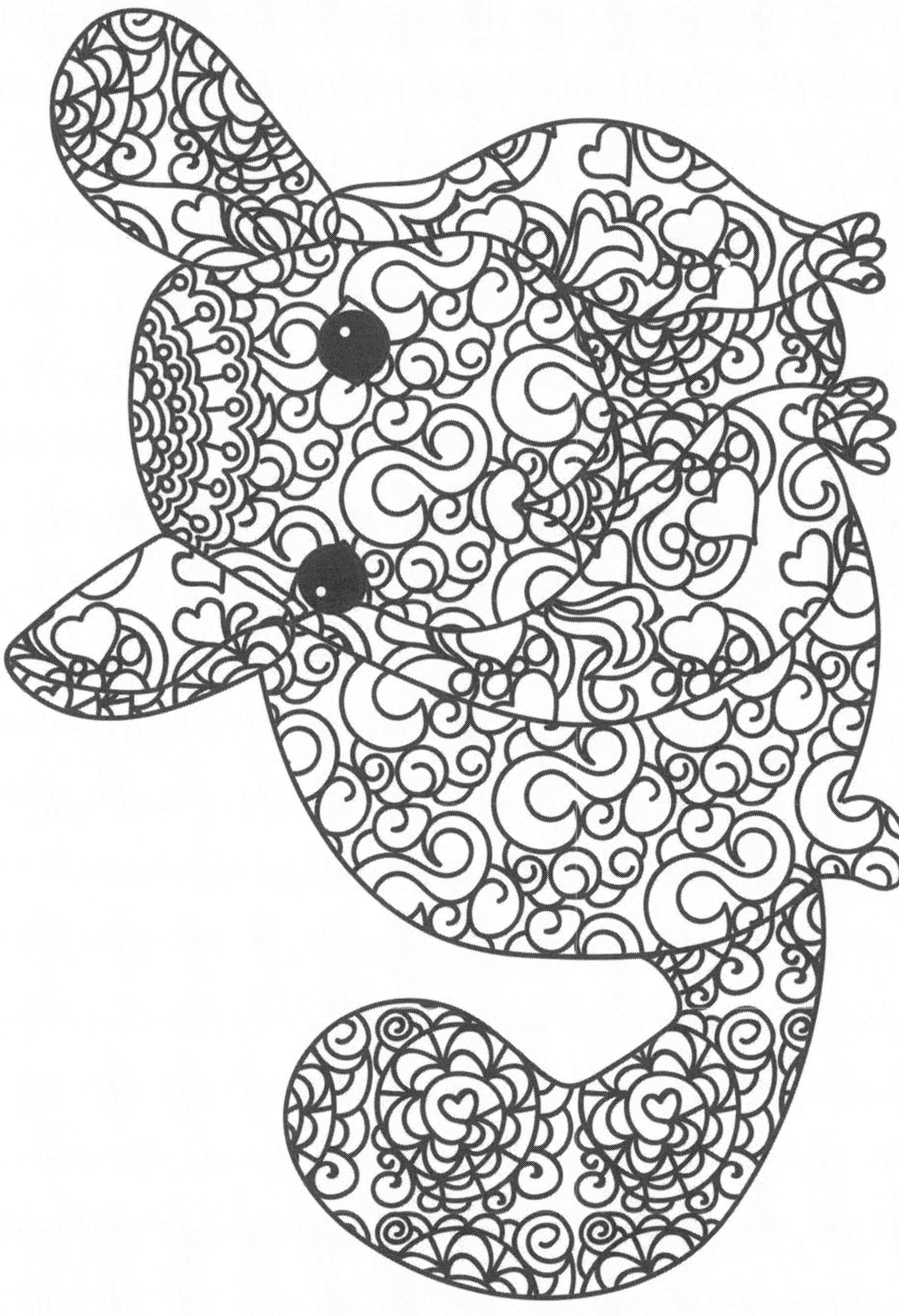

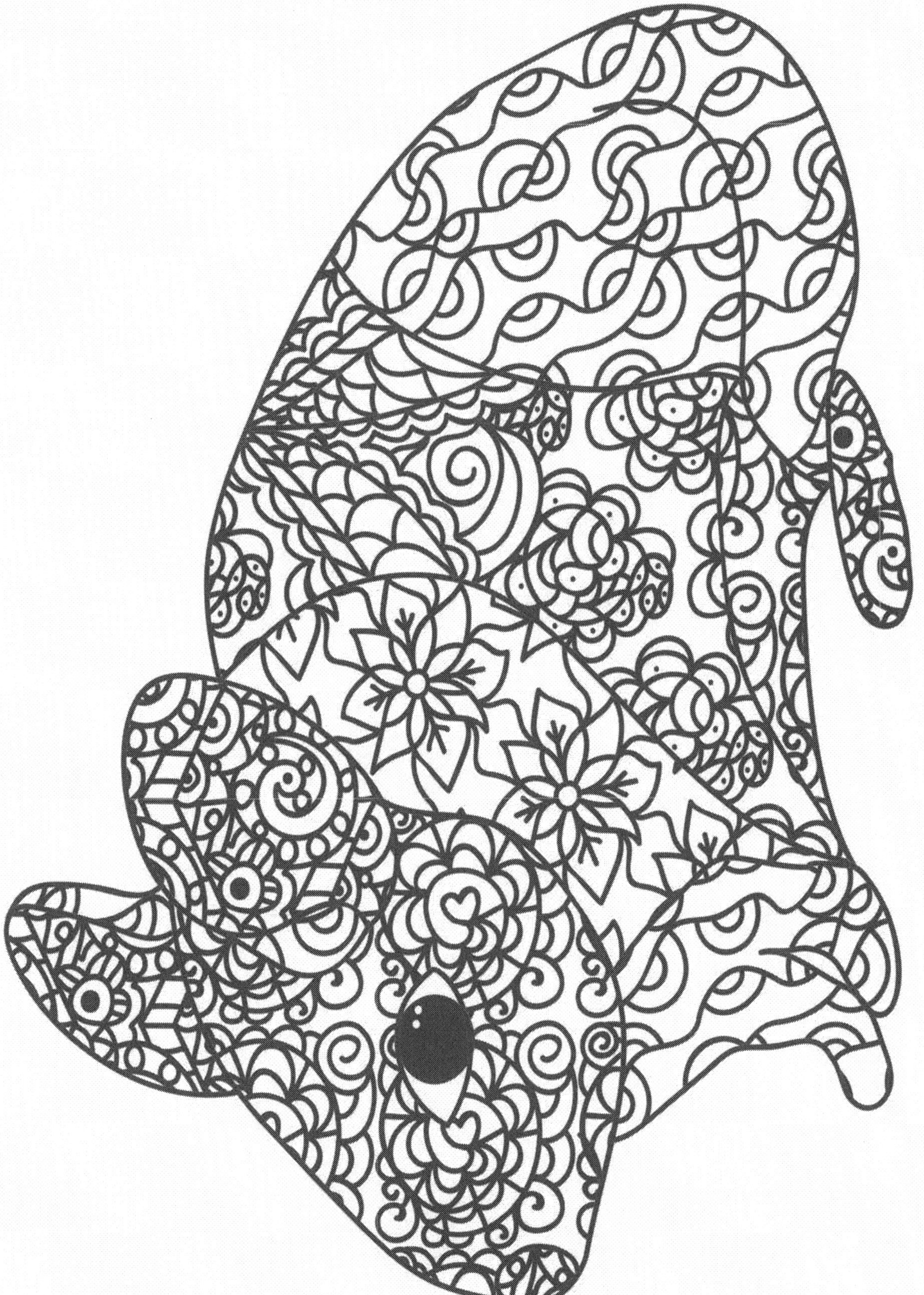

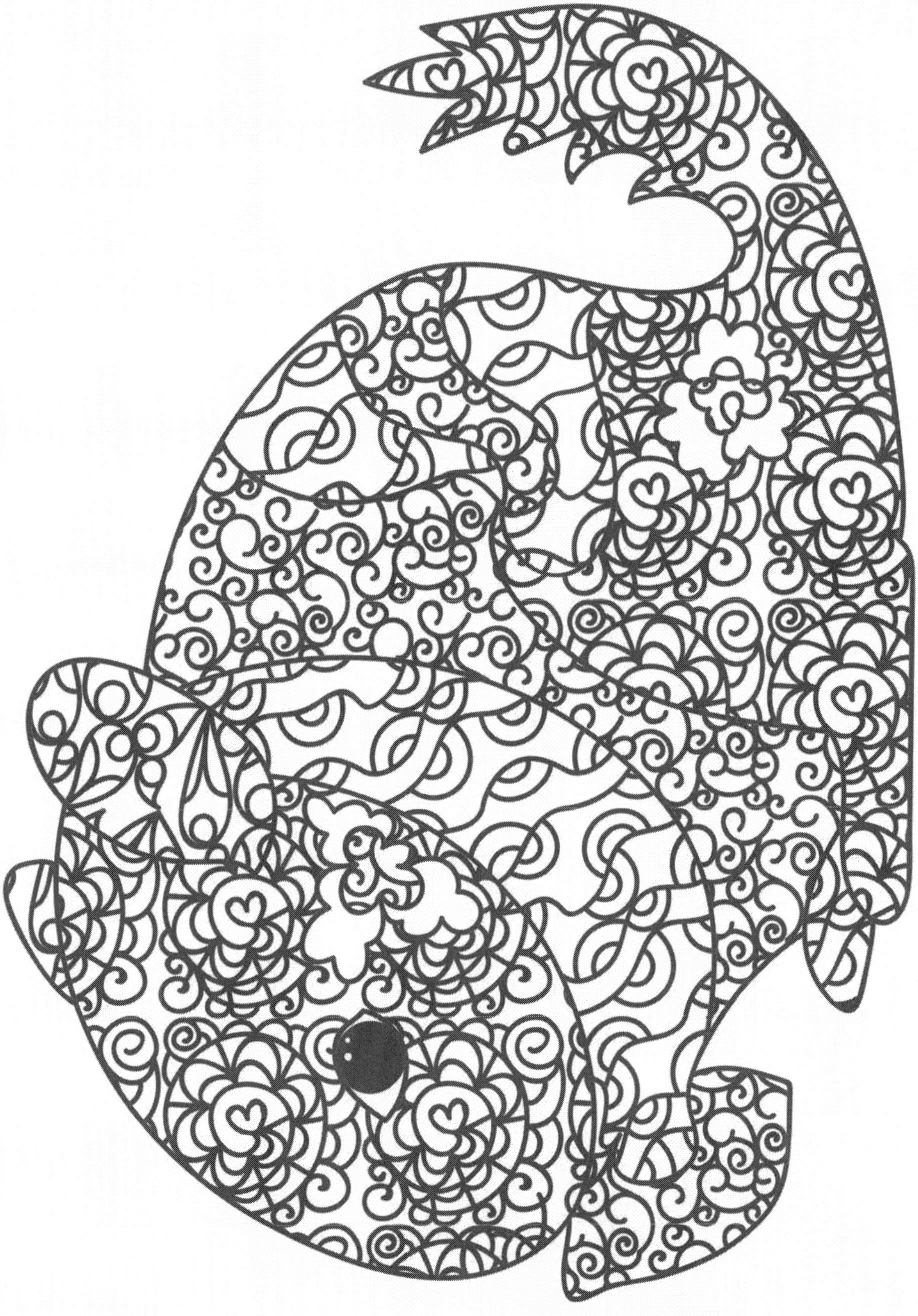

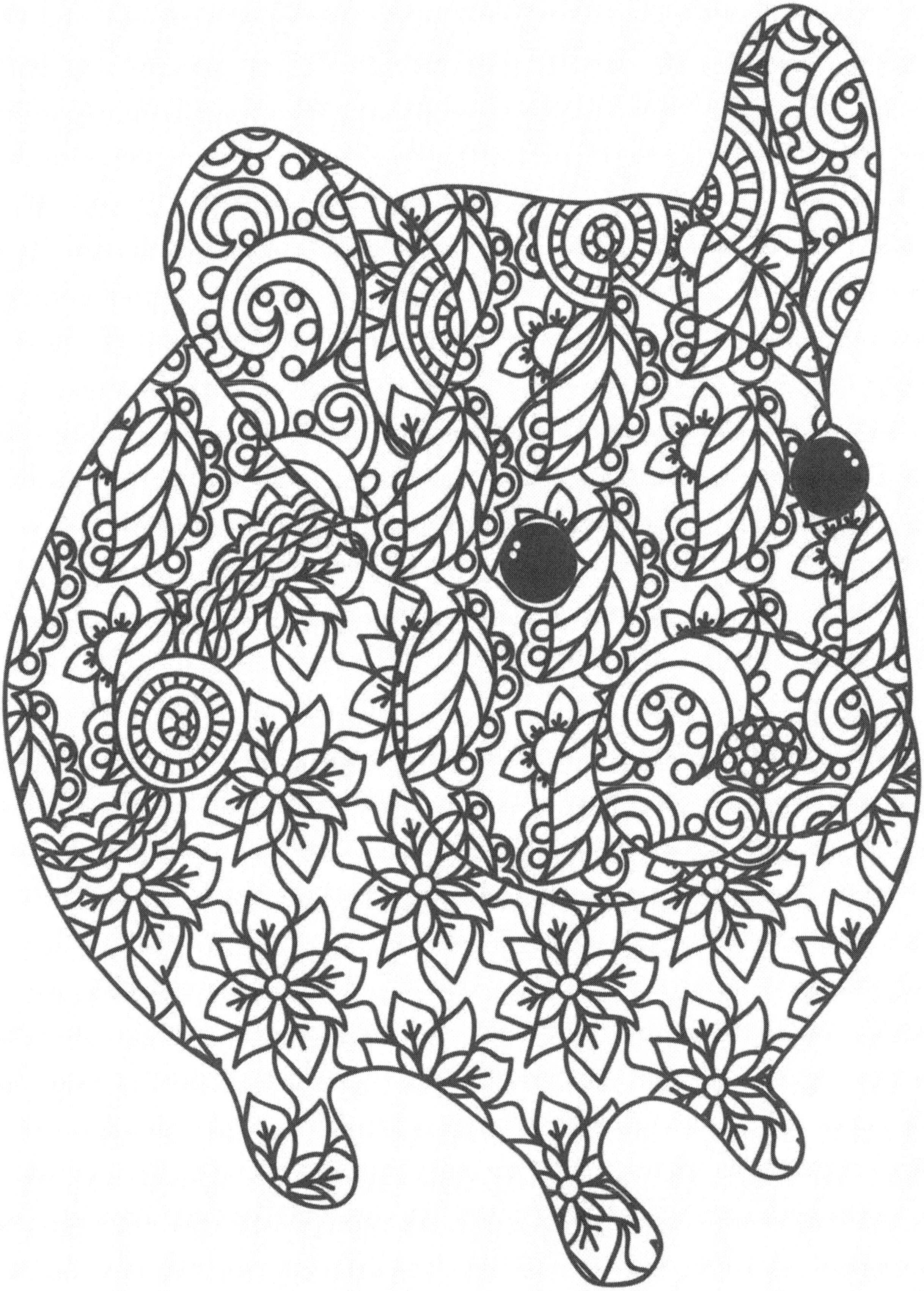

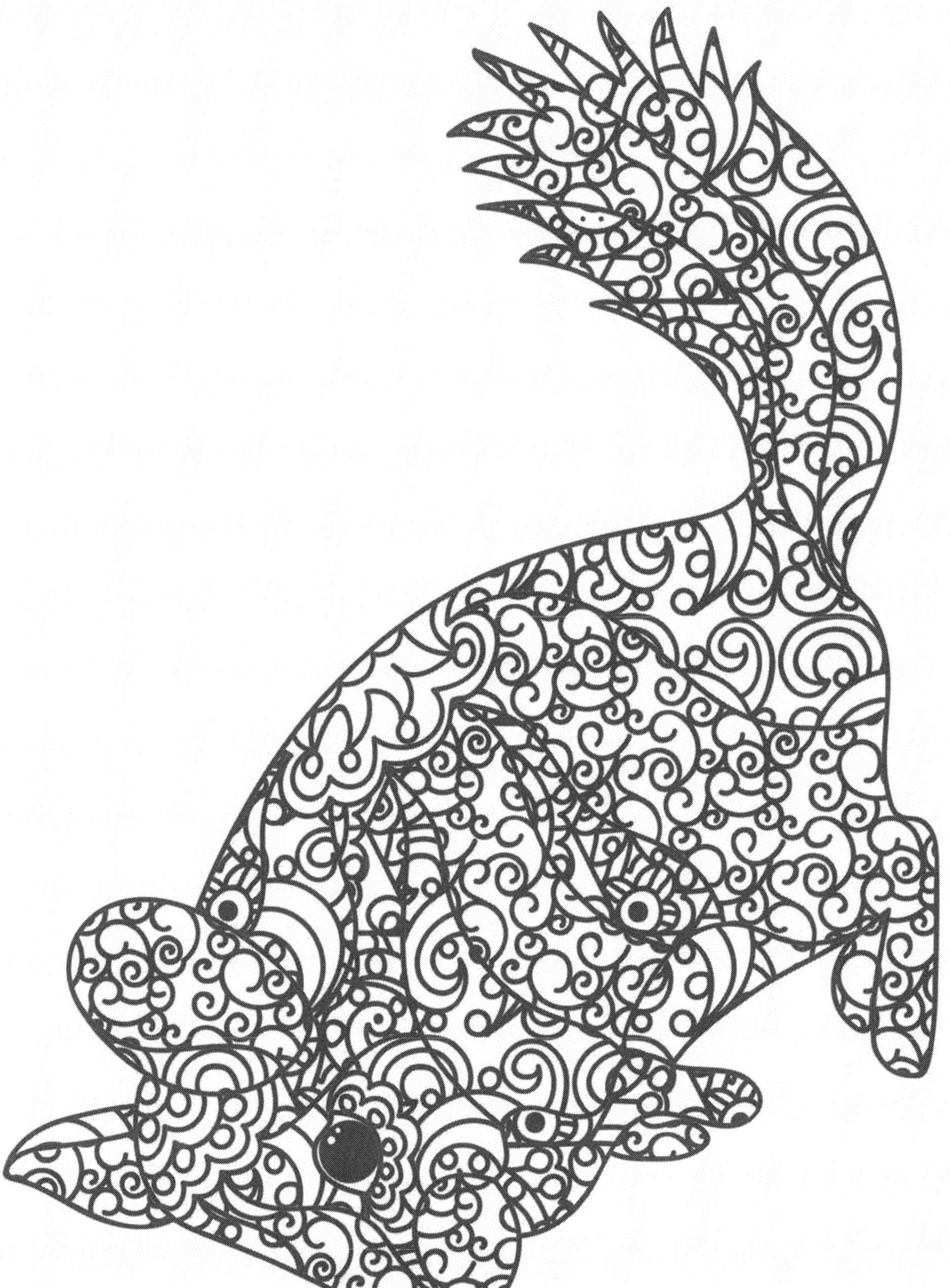

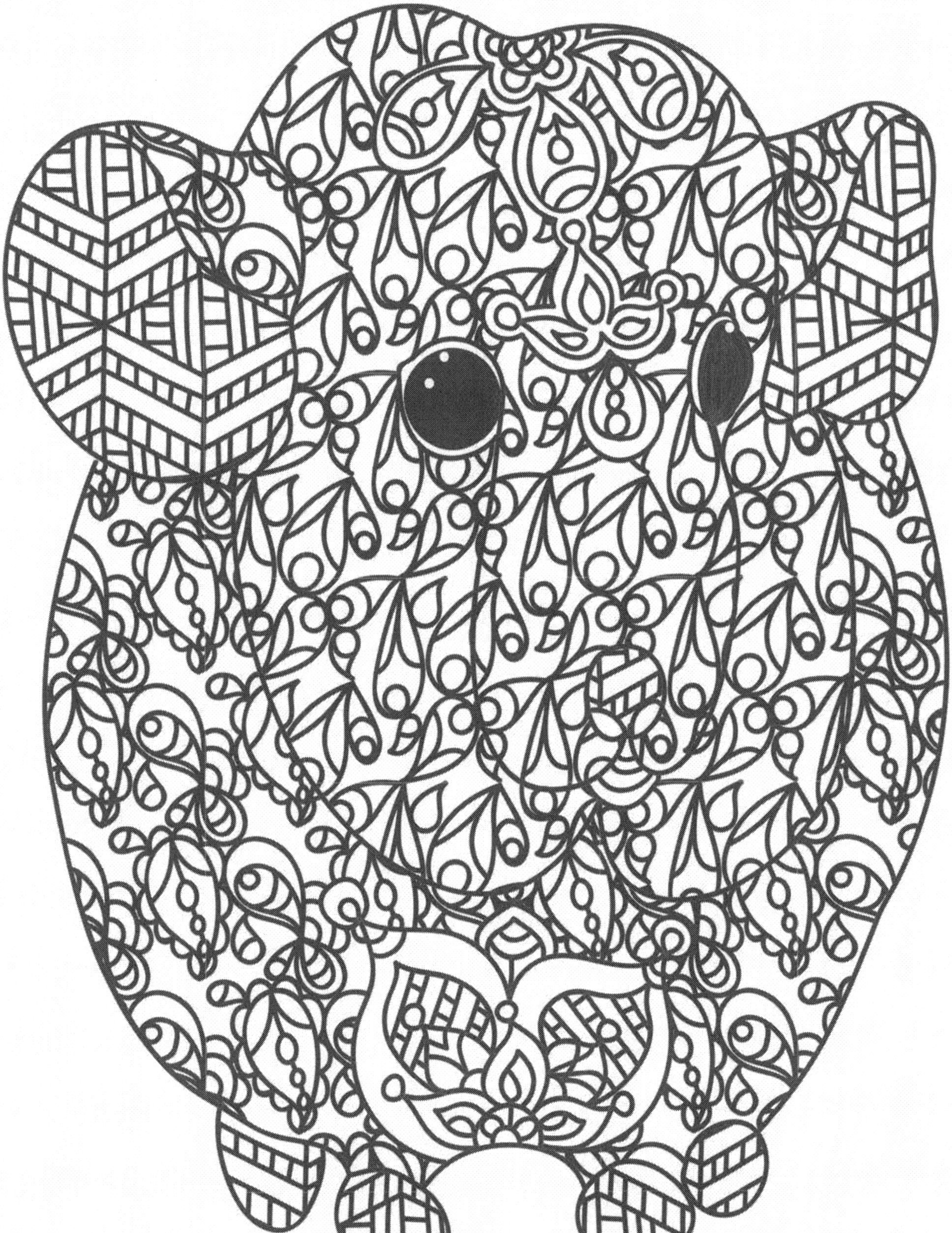

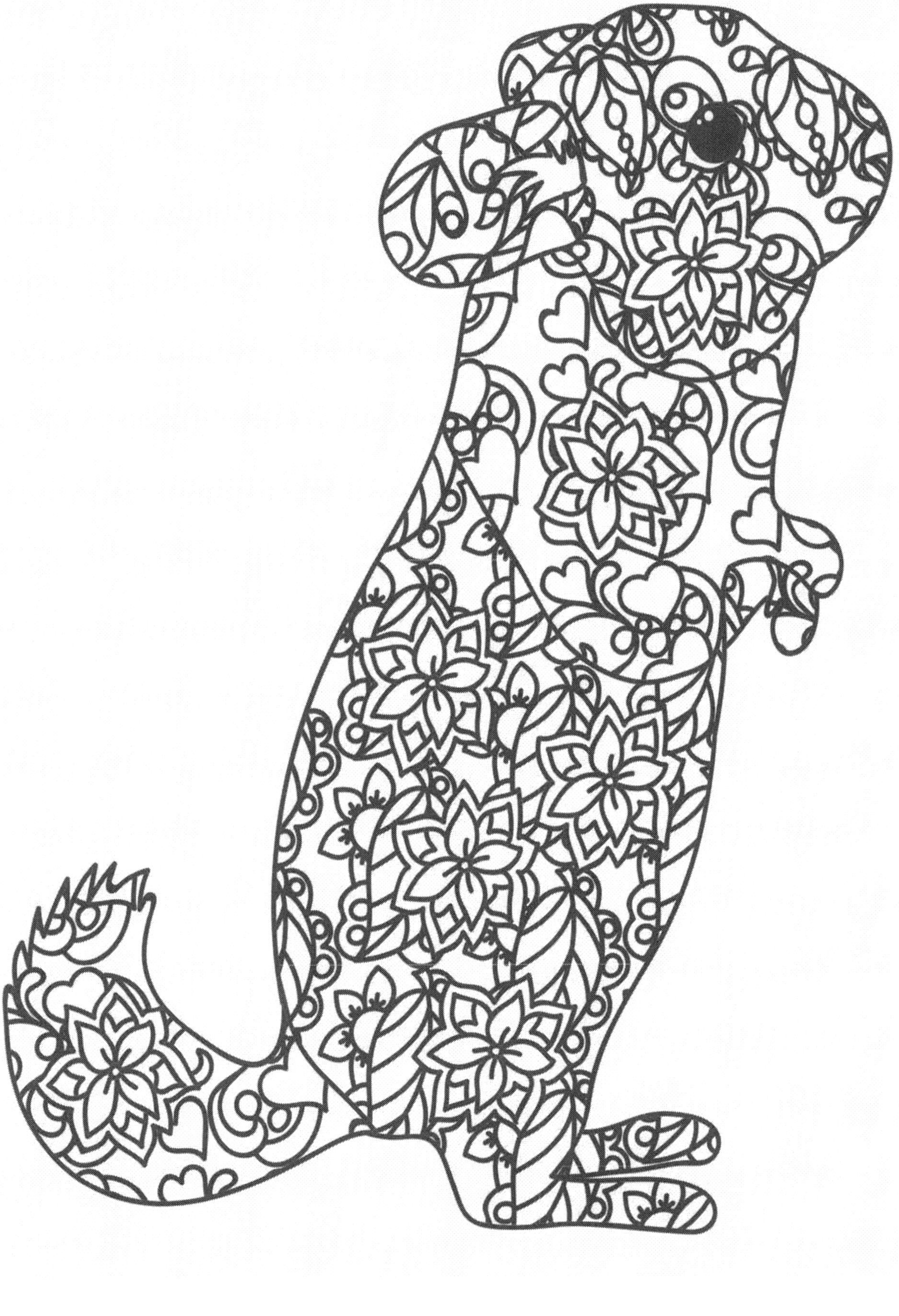

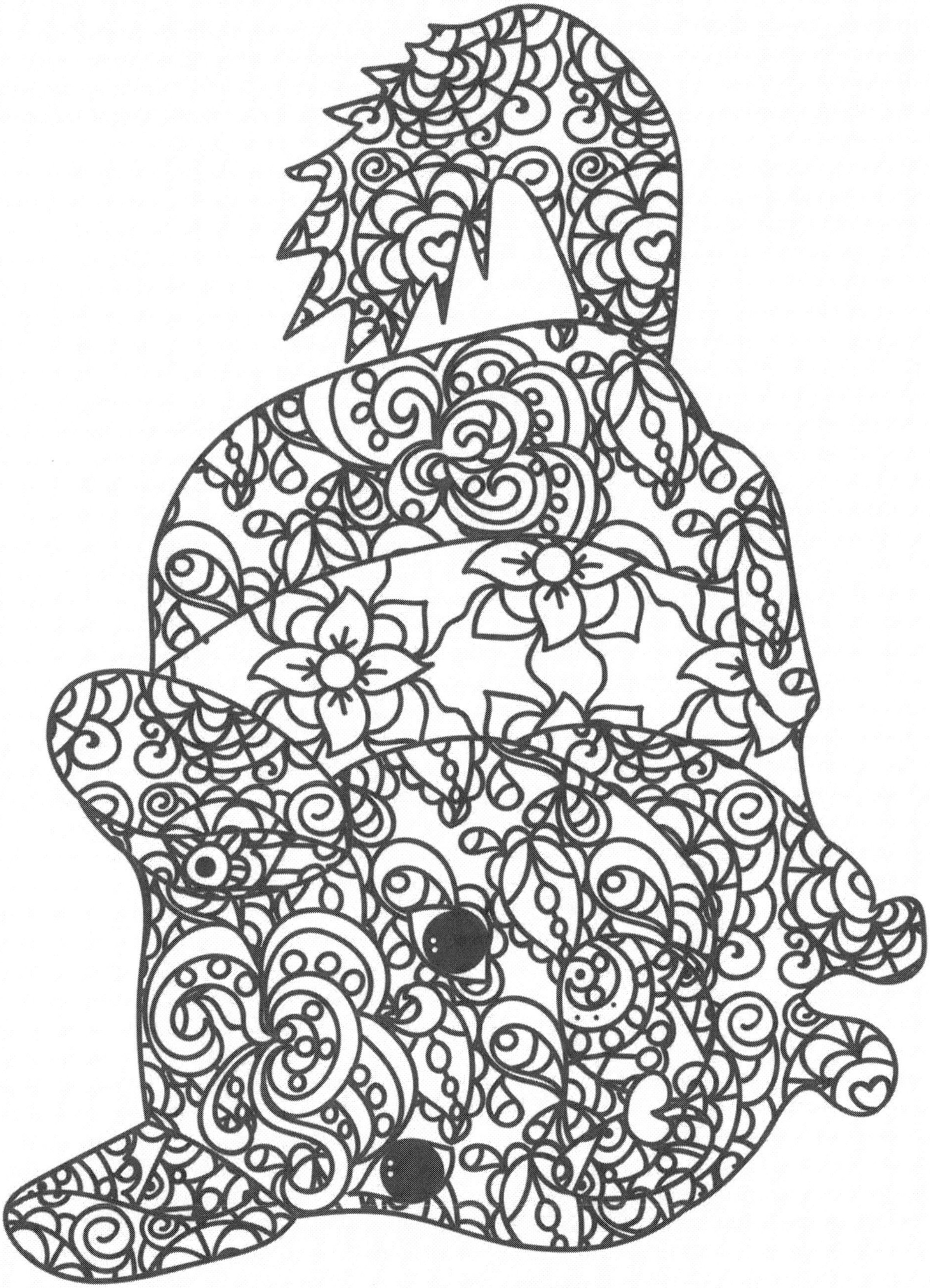

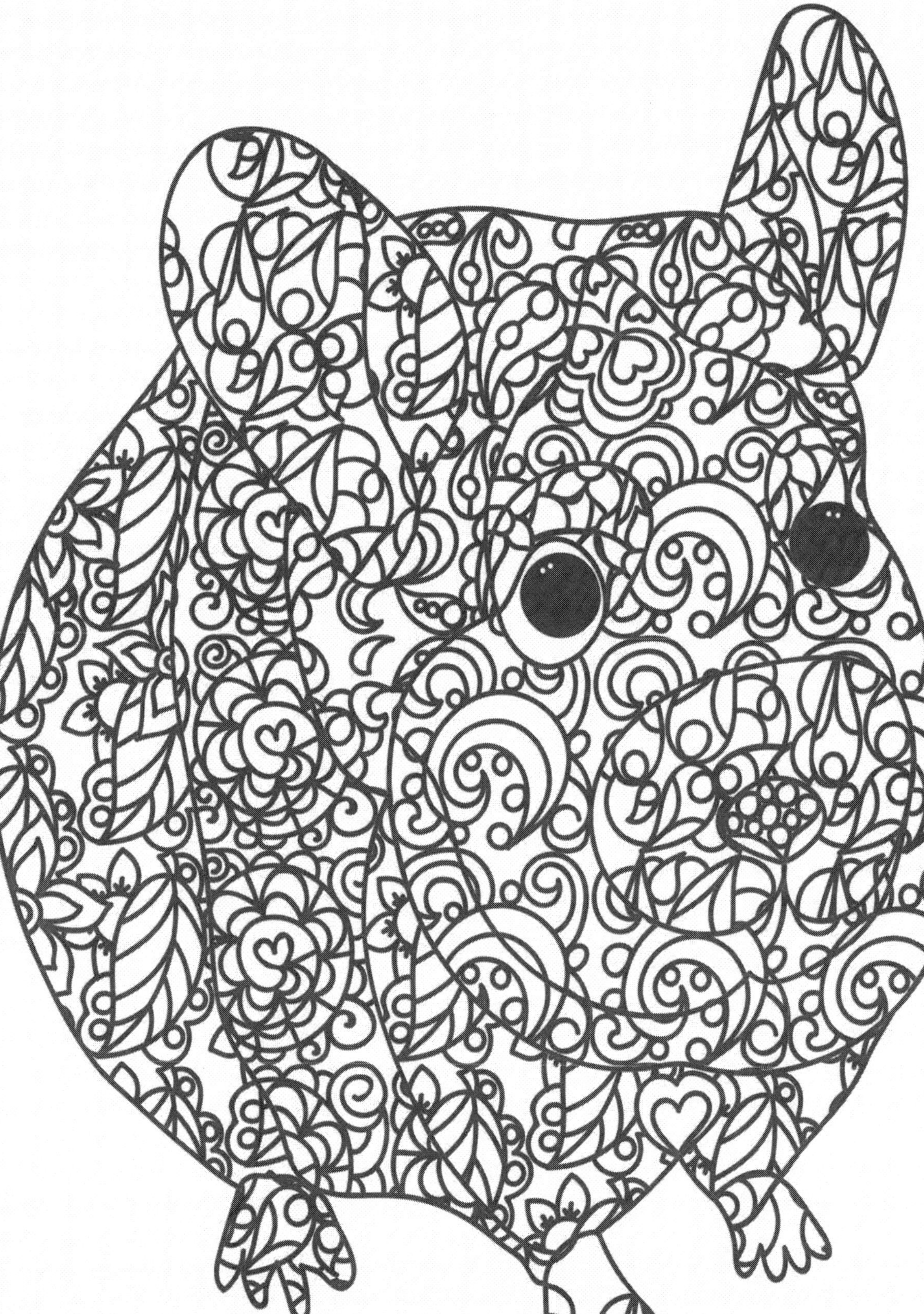

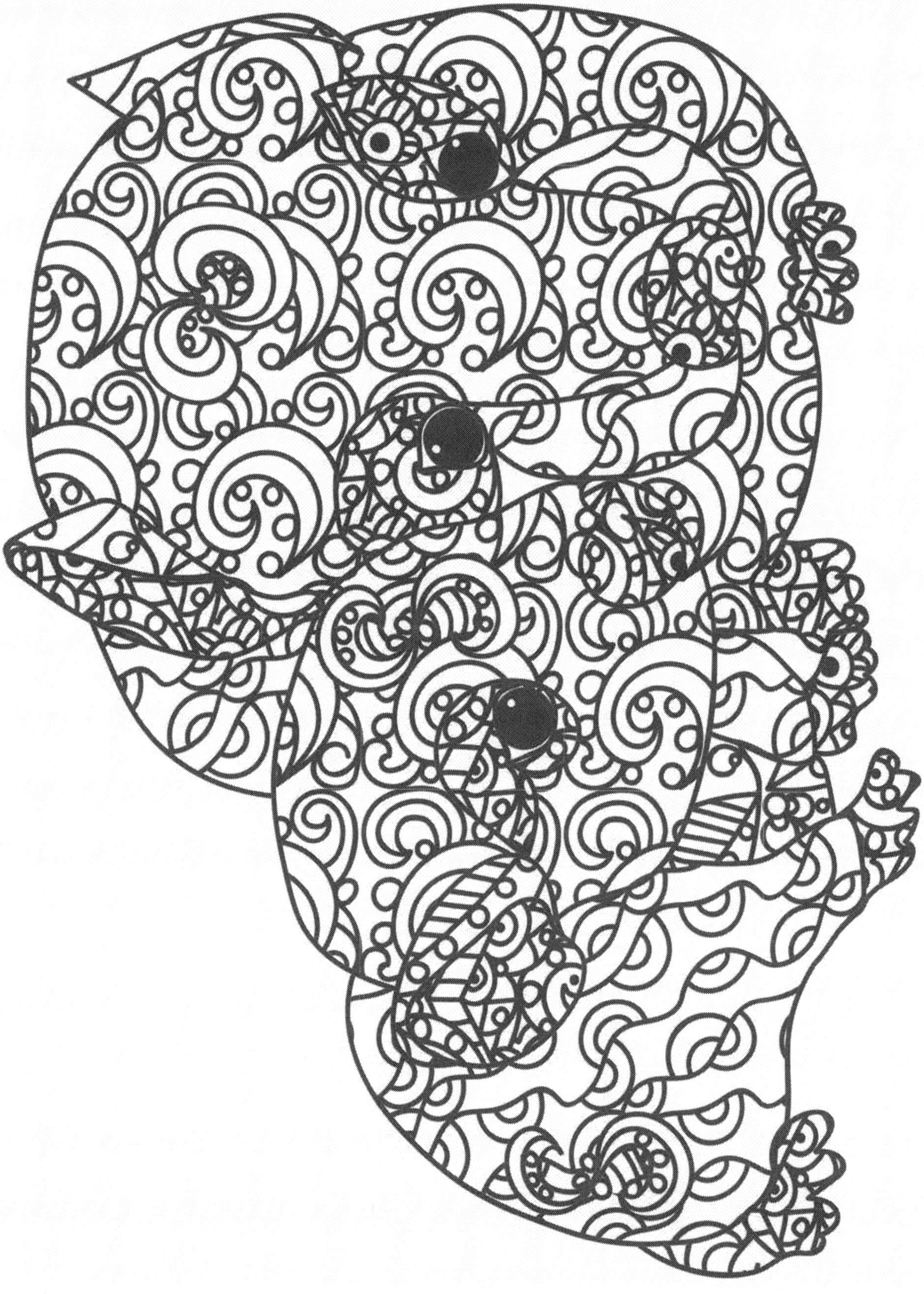

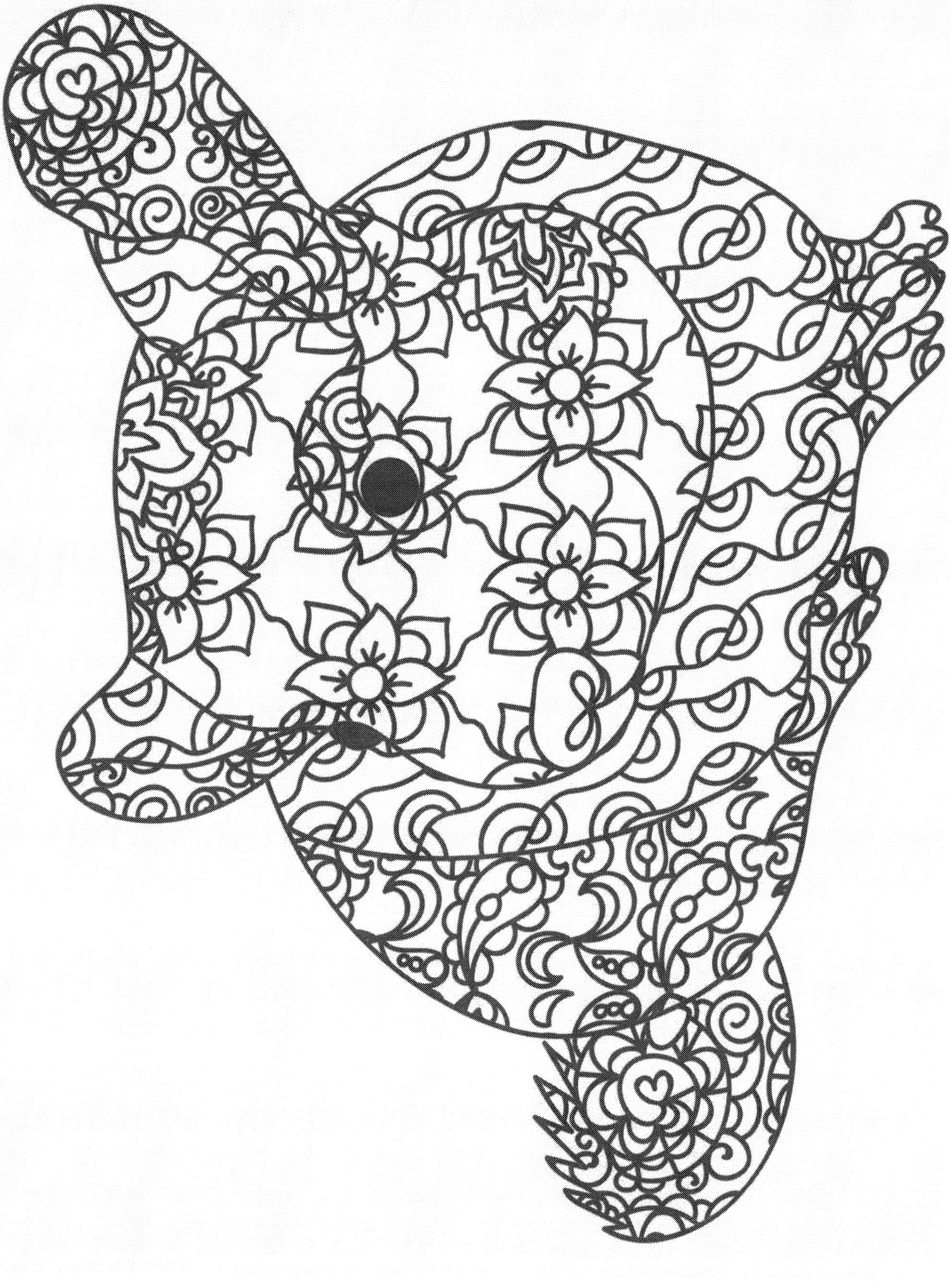

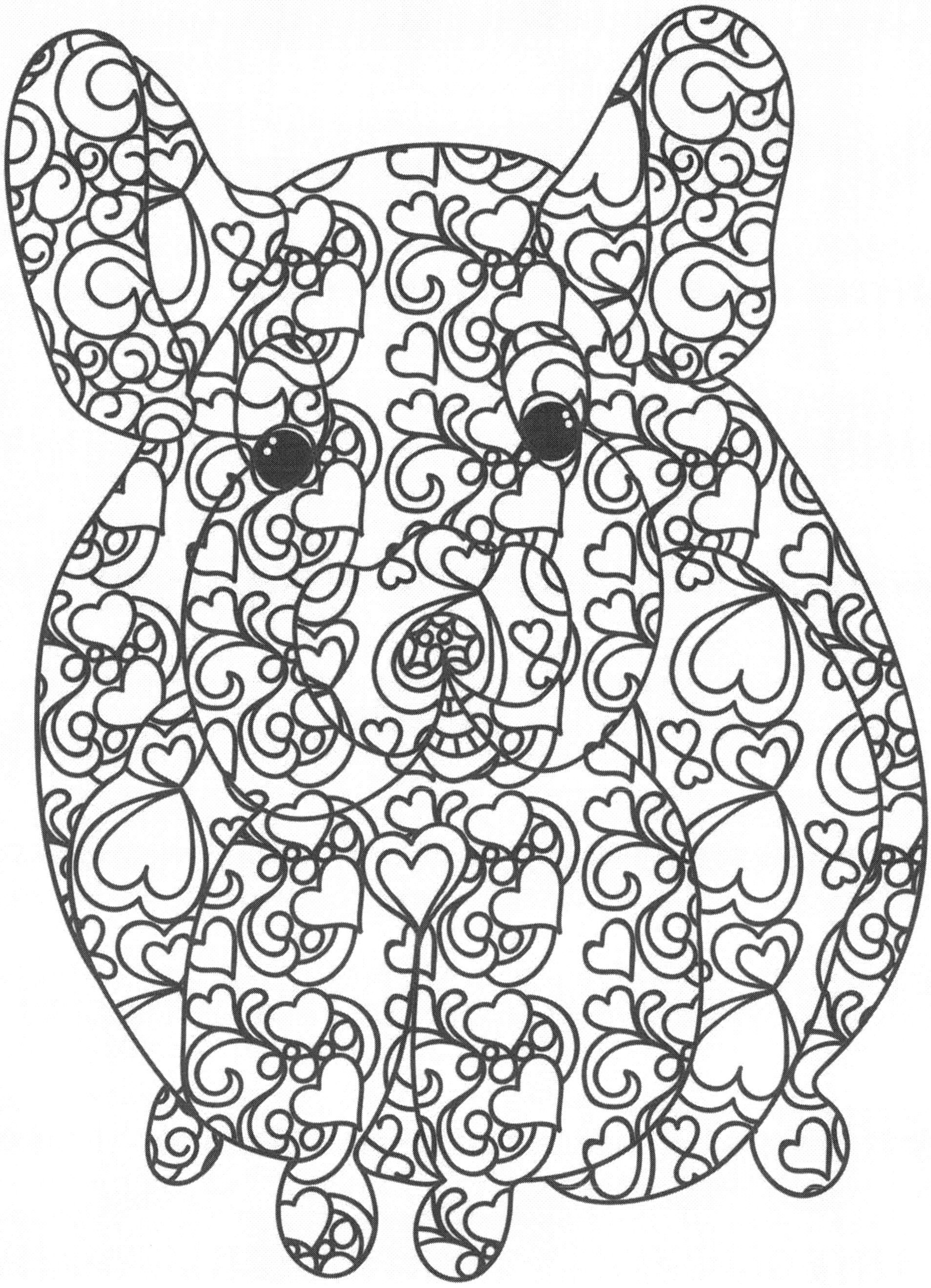

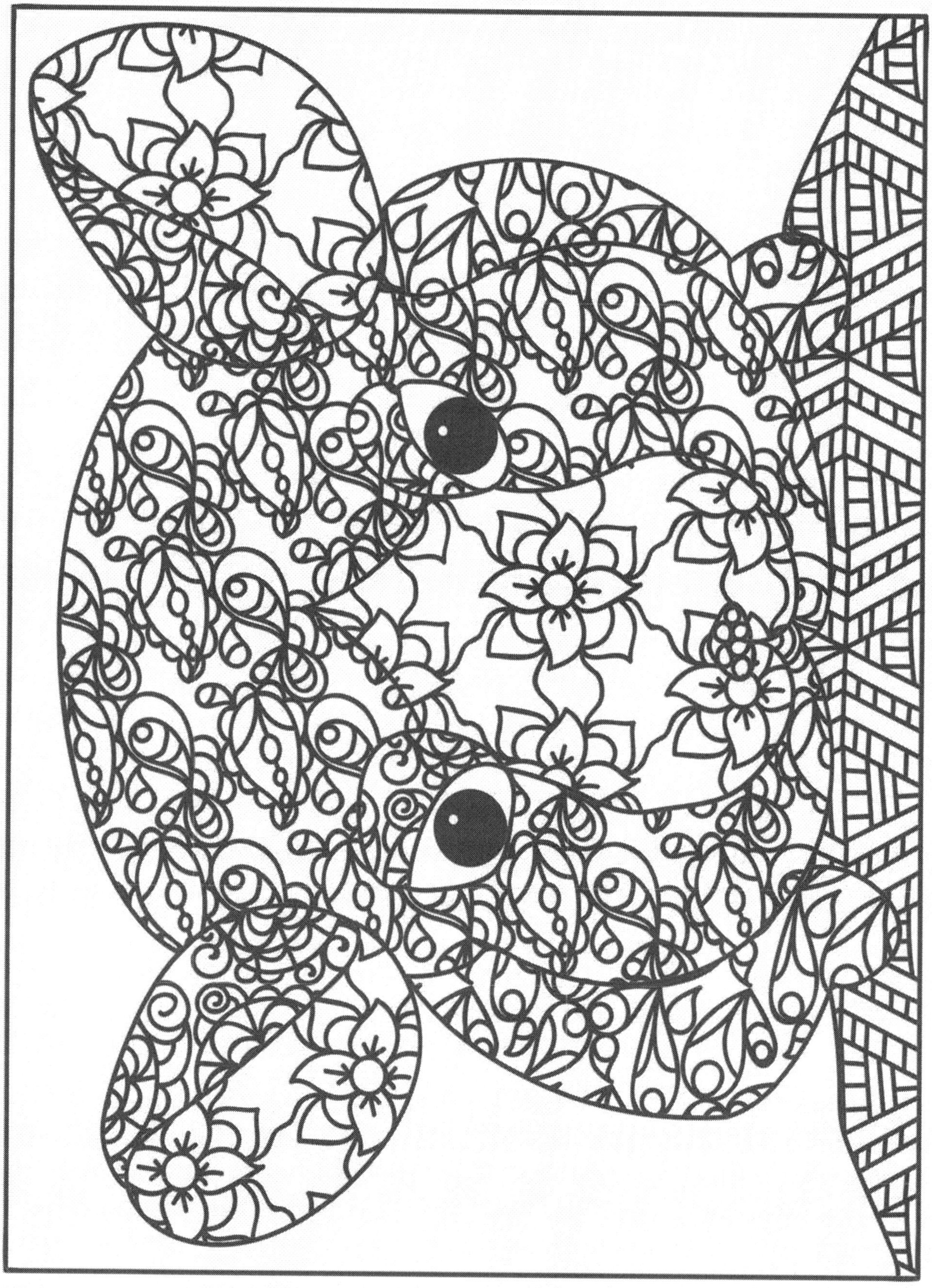

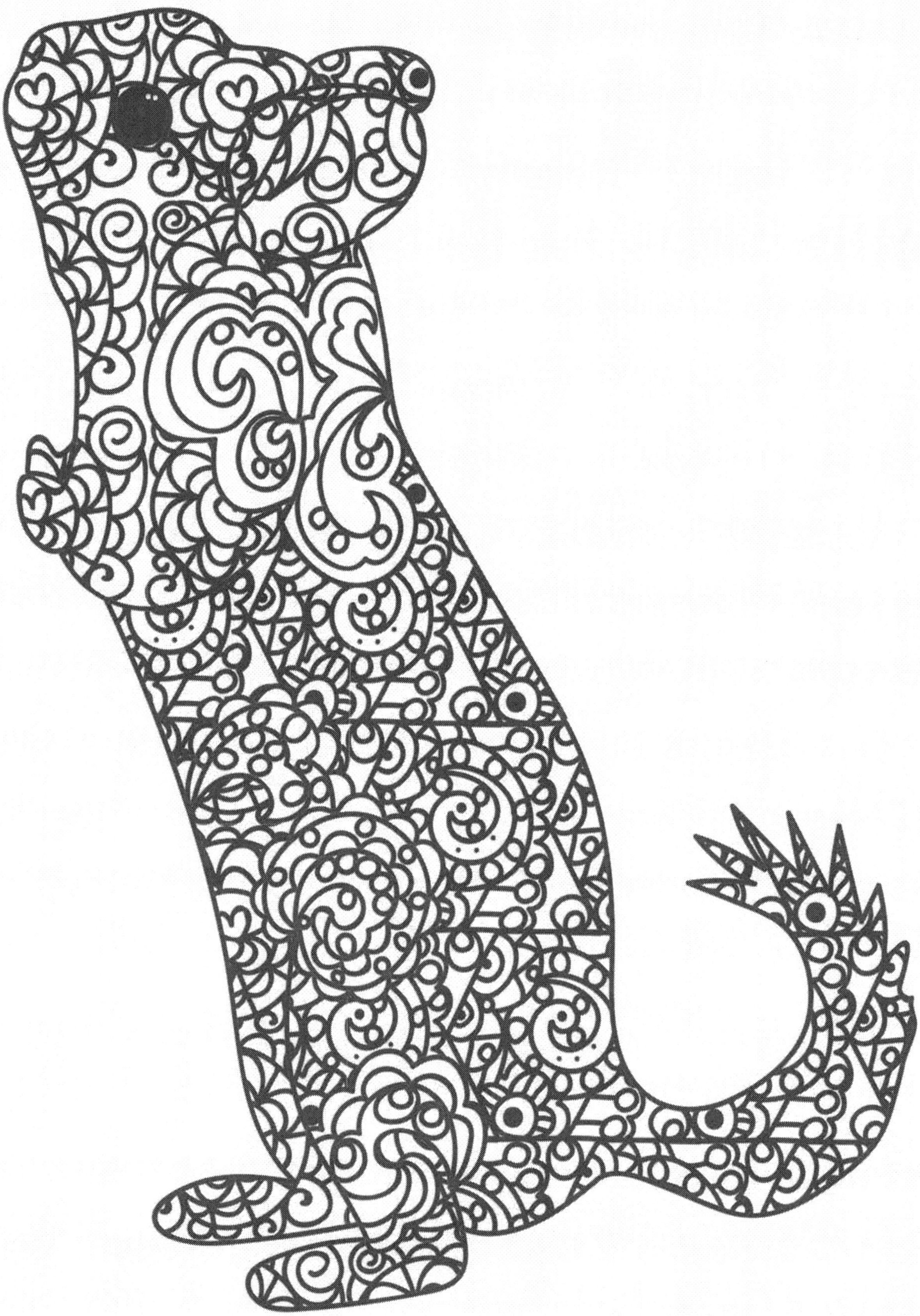

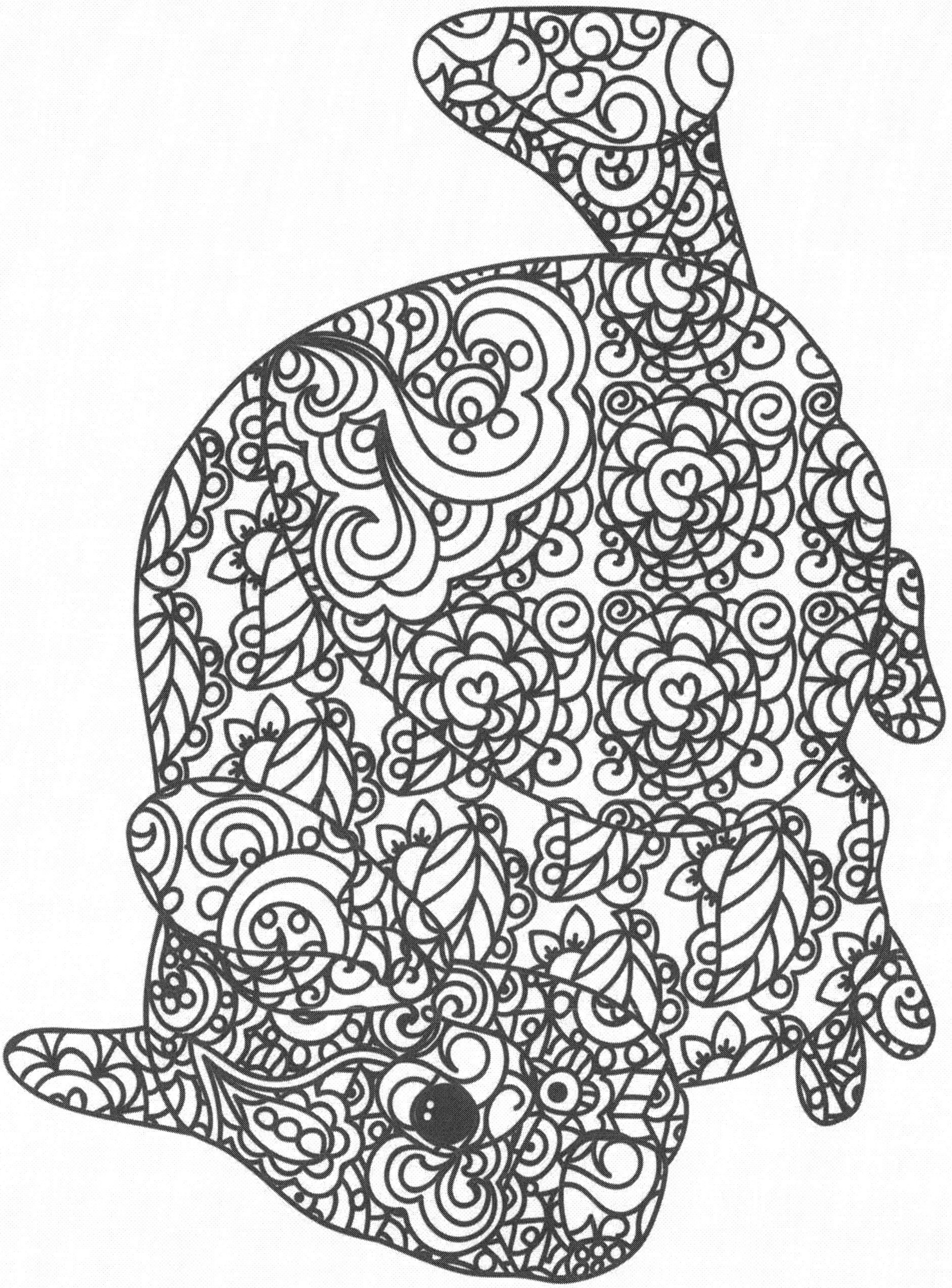

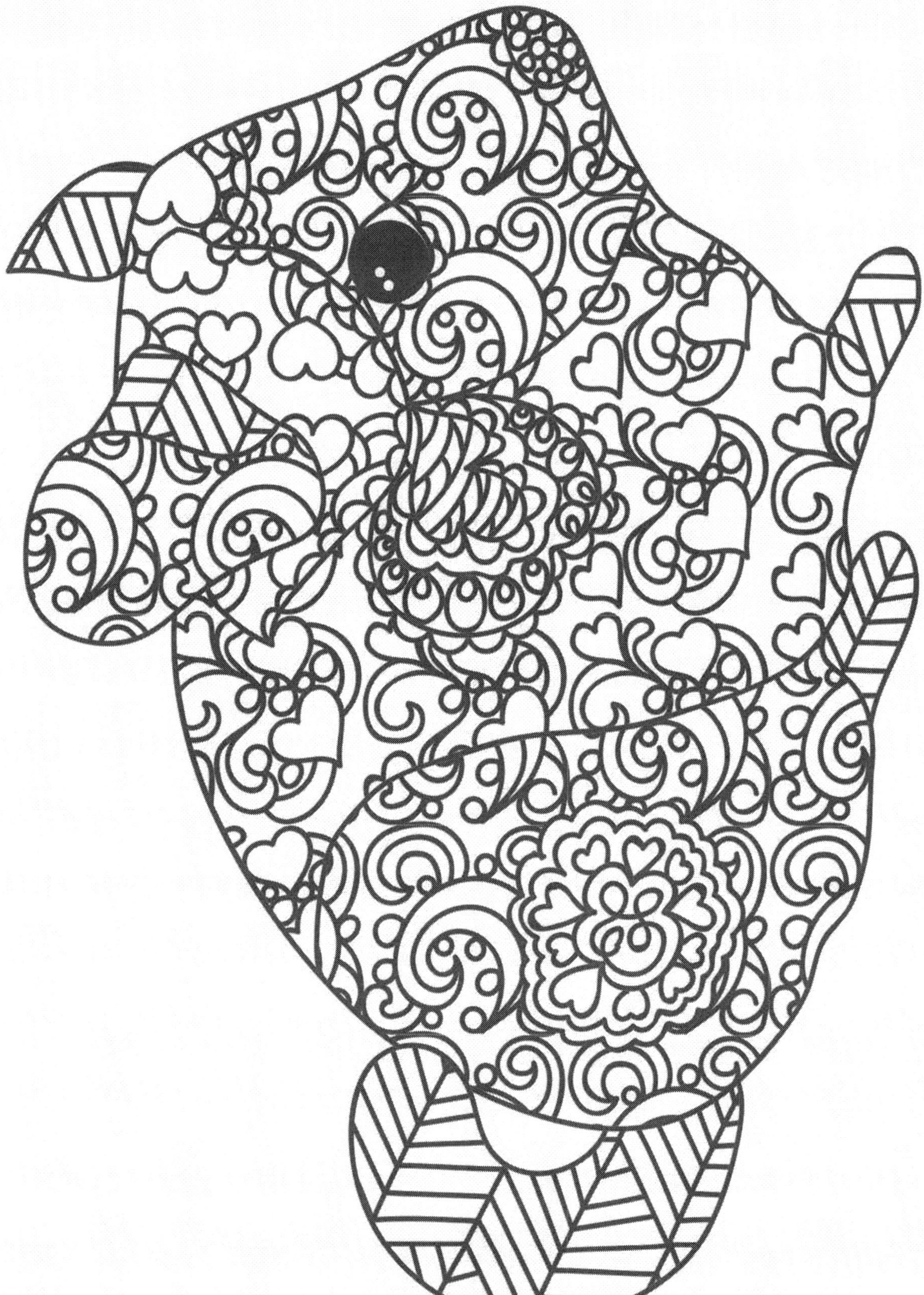

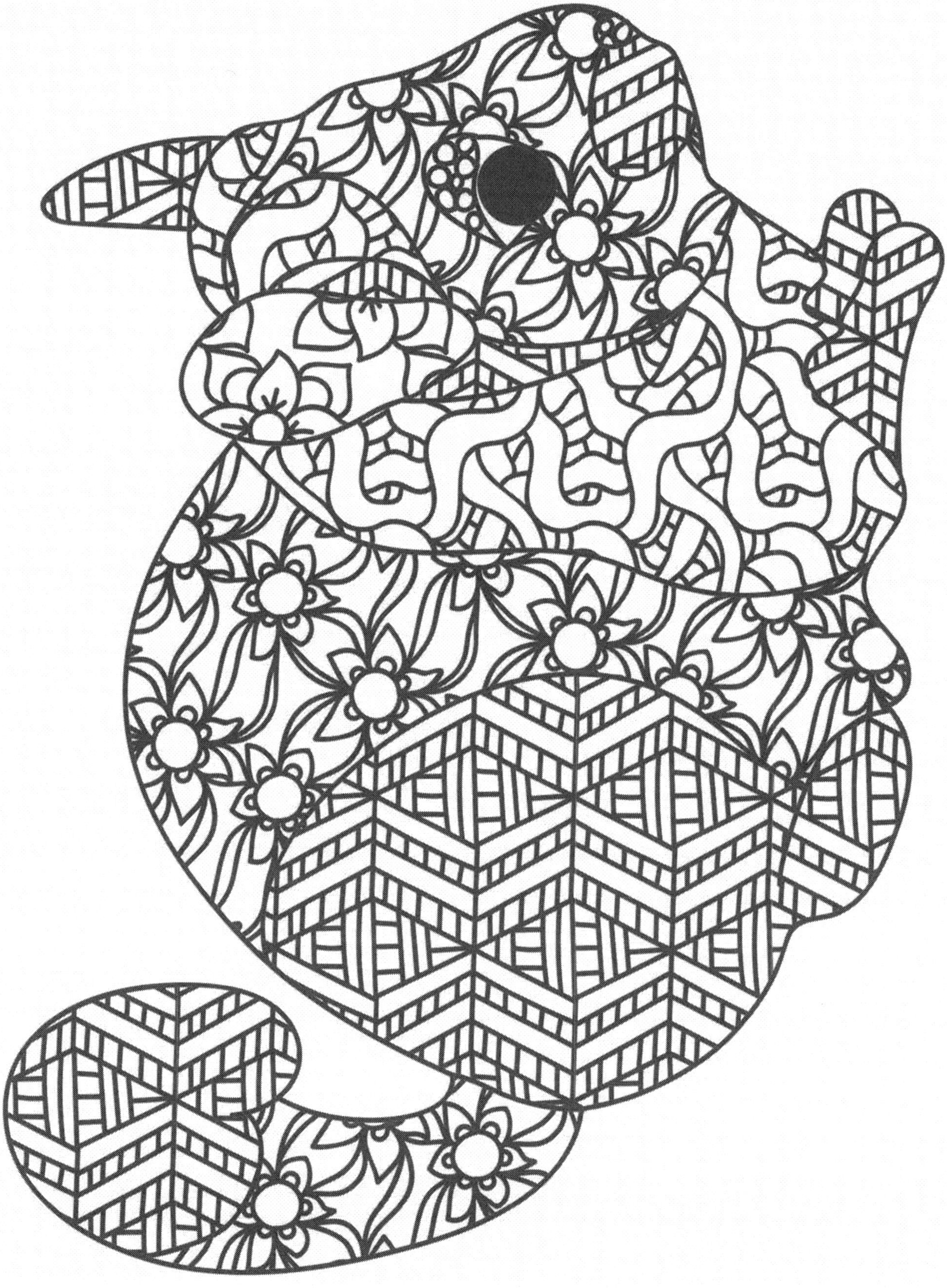

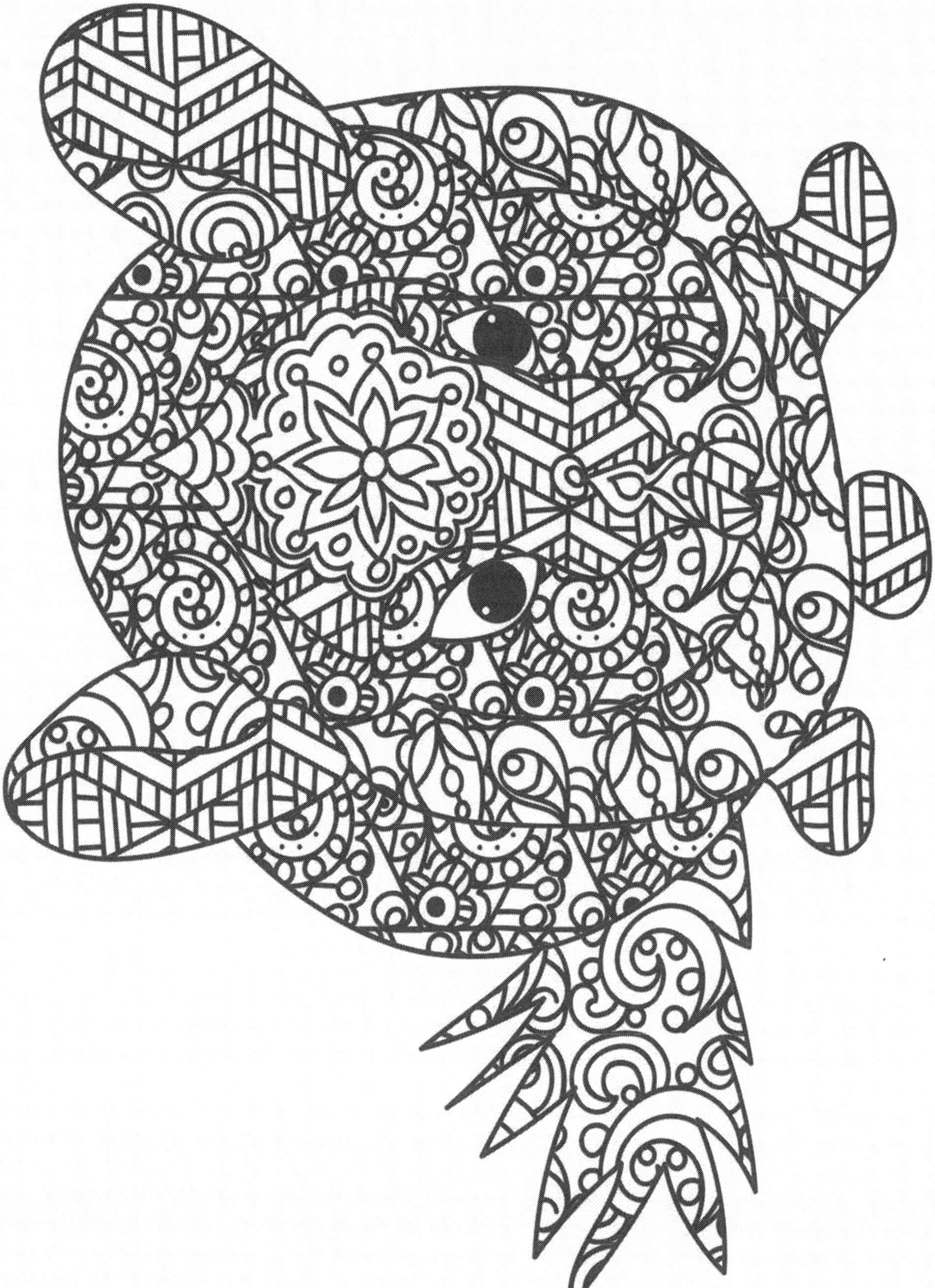

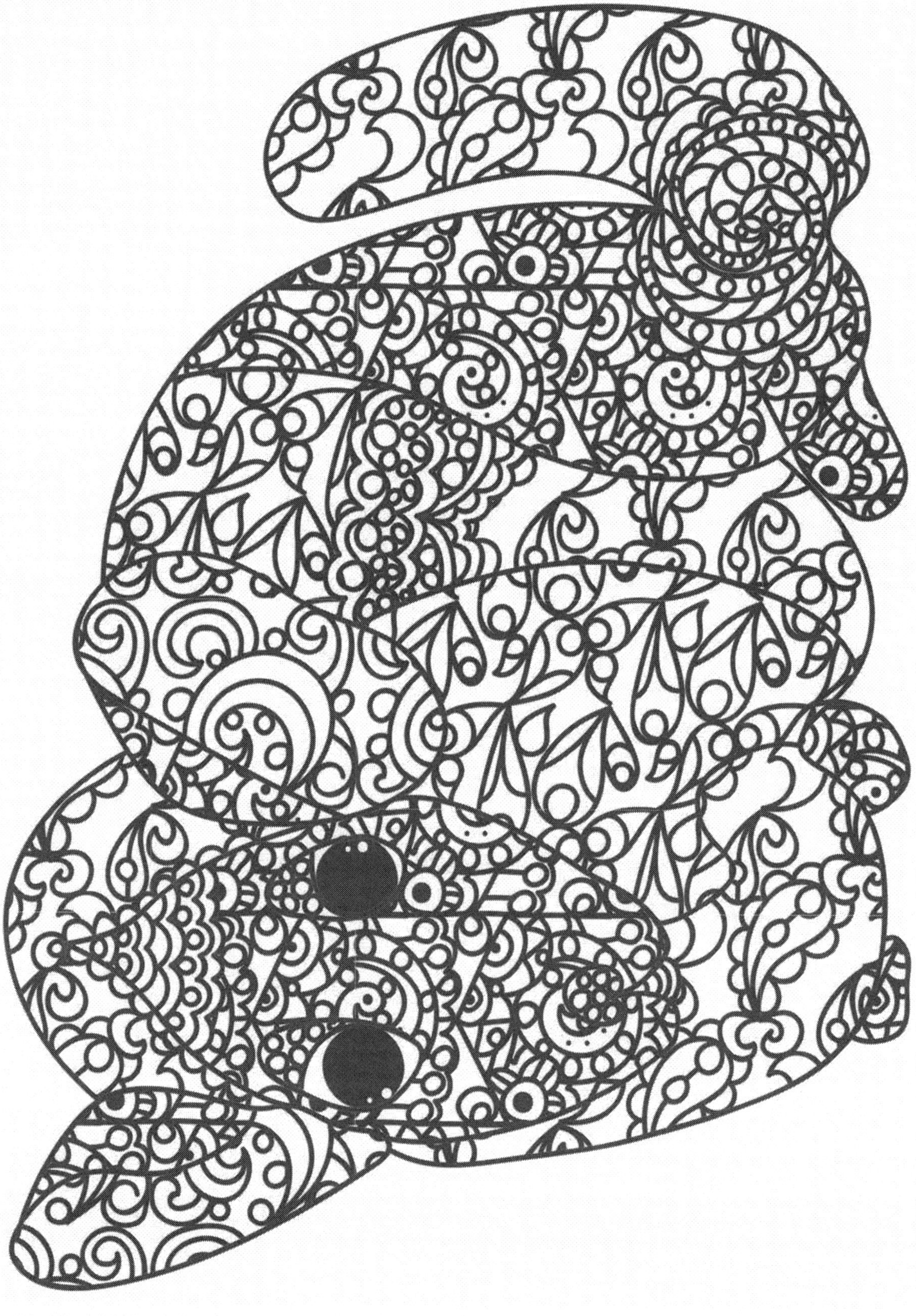

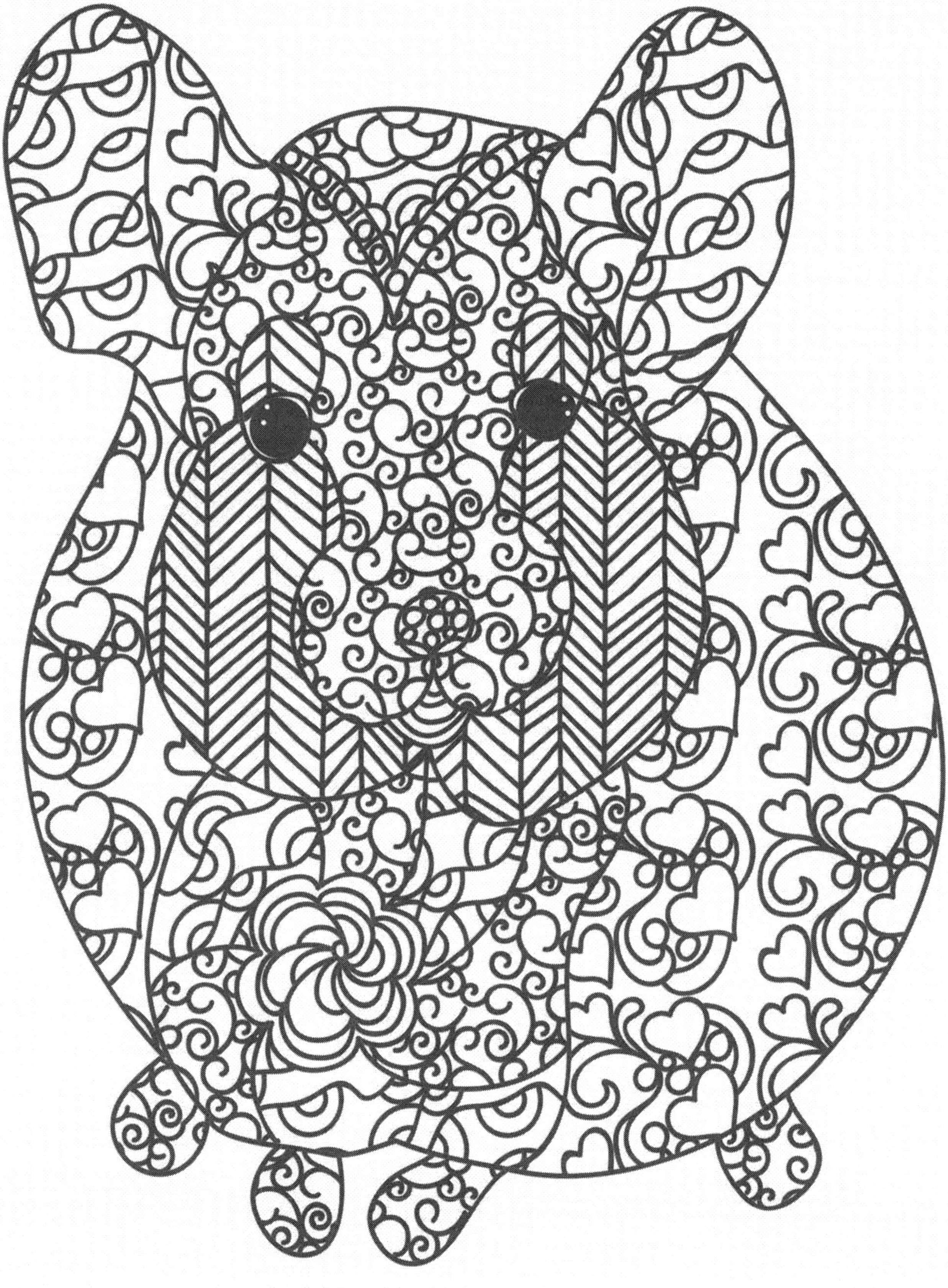

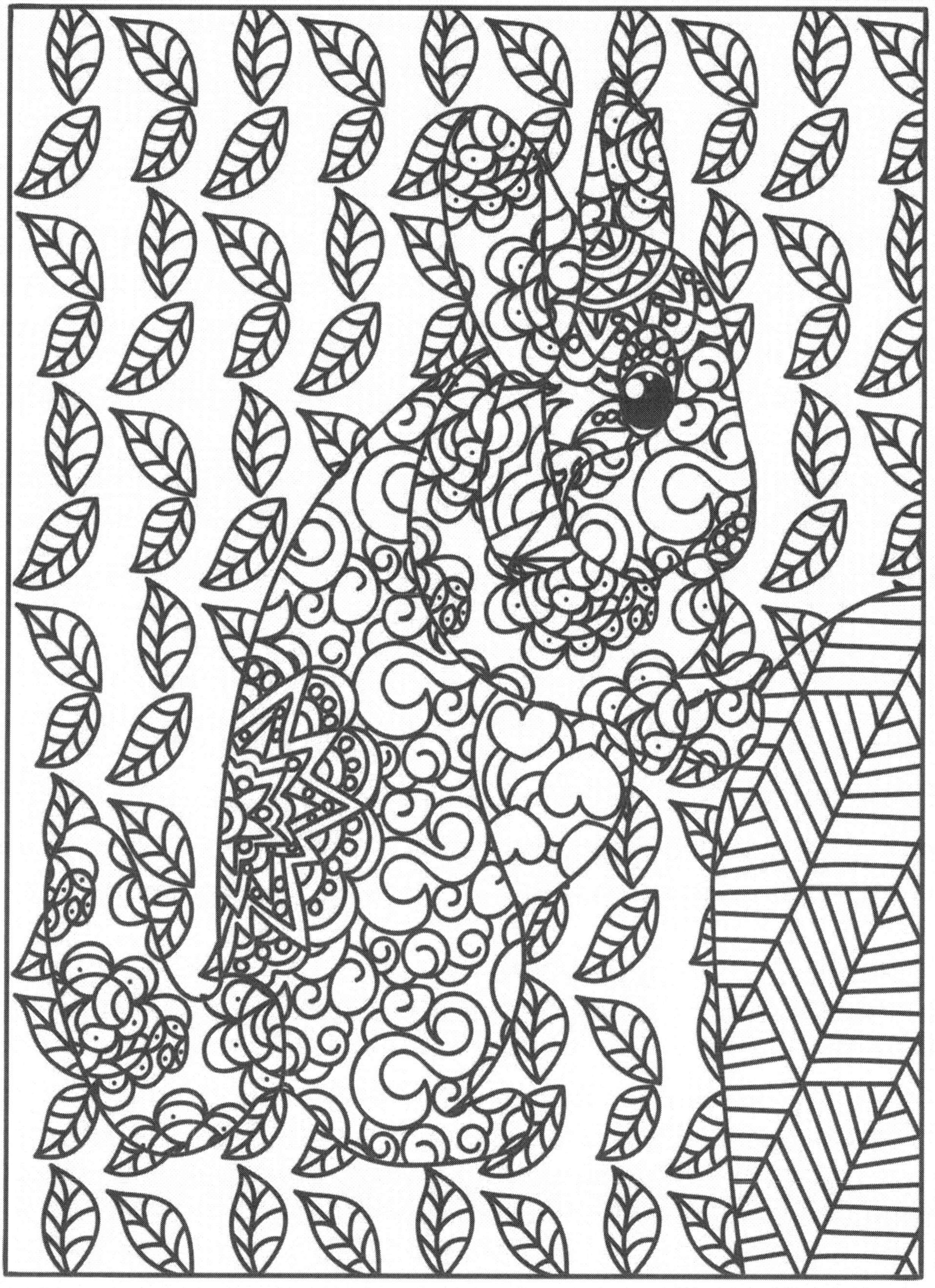

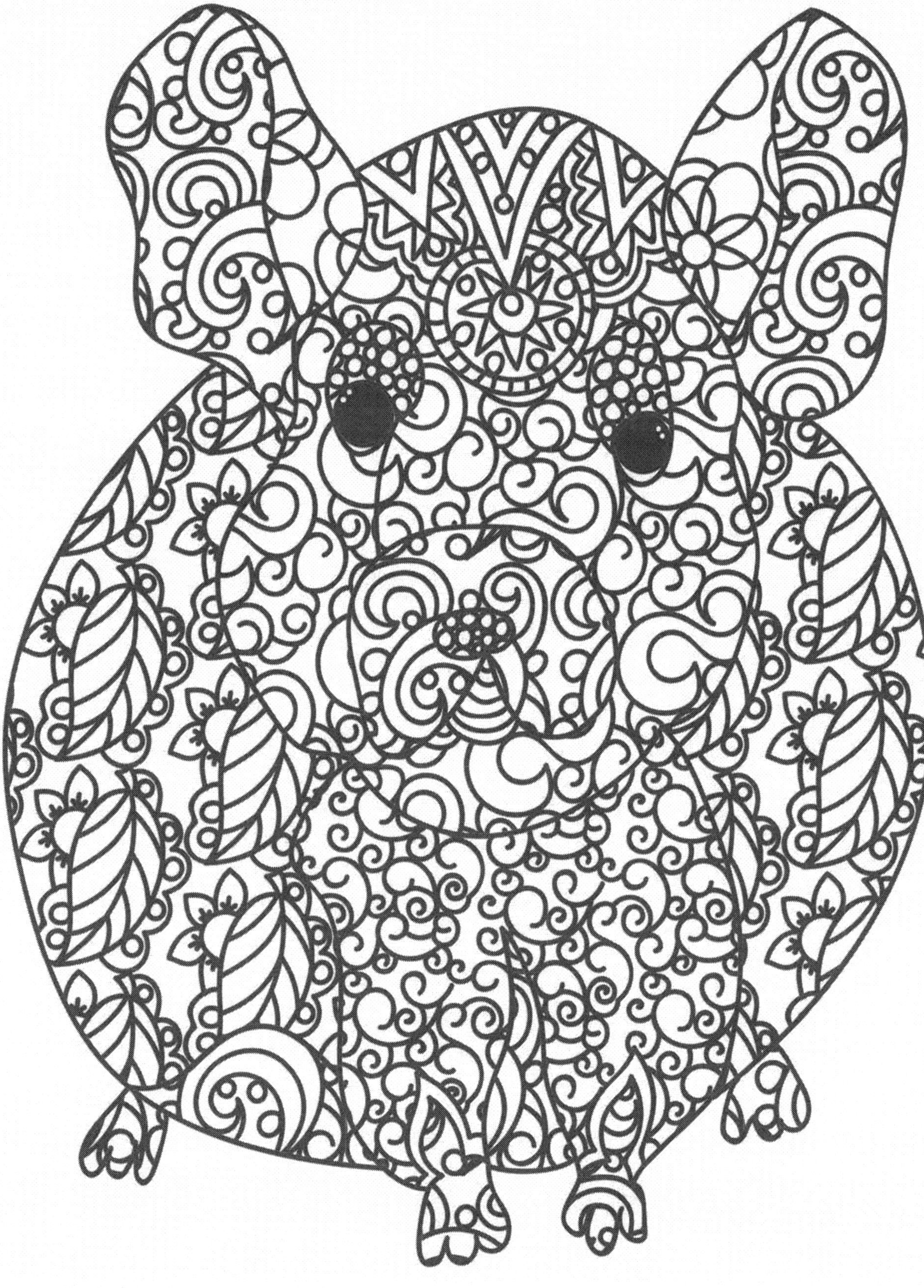

COLOR TEST PAGE

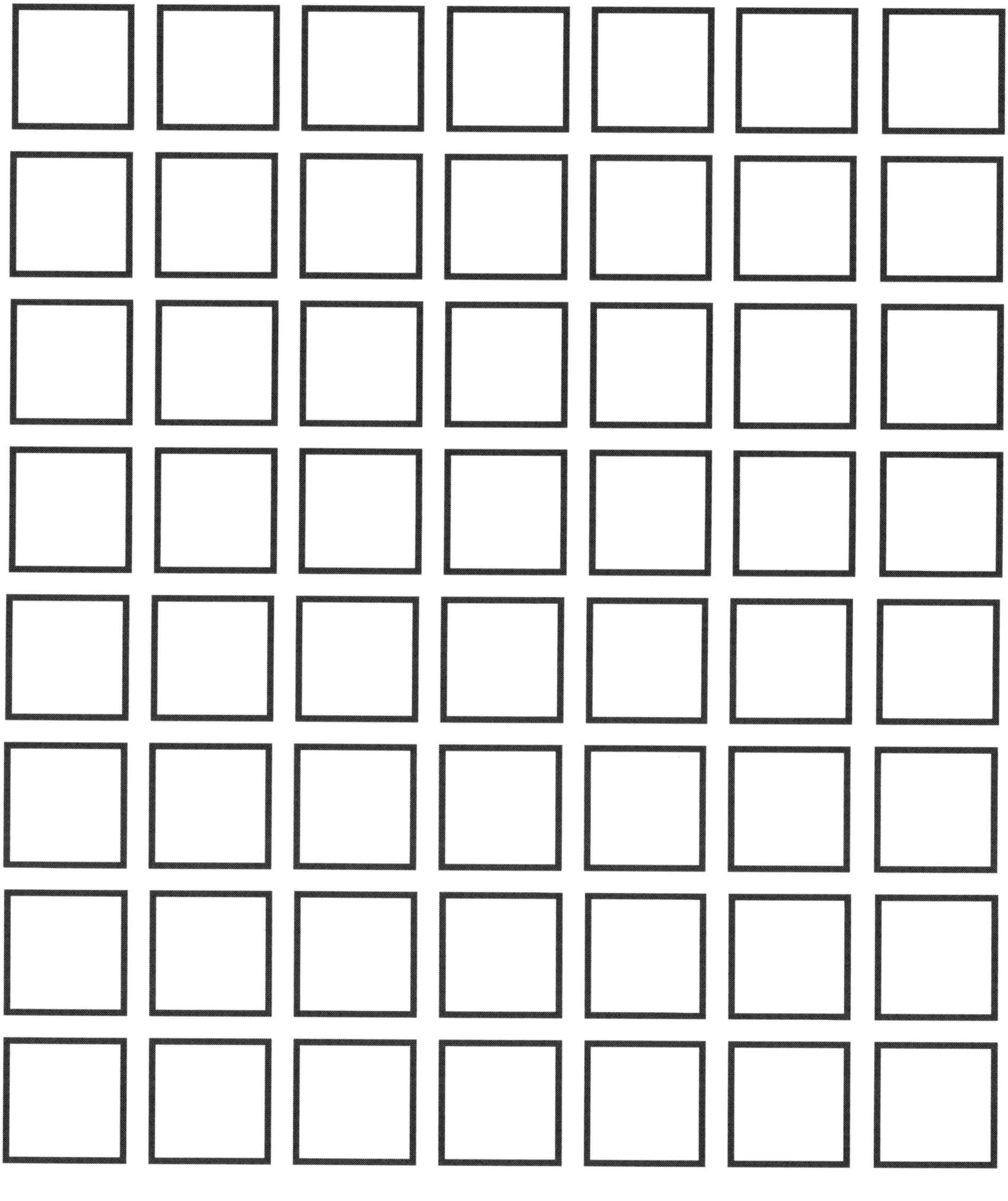

COLOR TEST PAGE

64281041R00038

Made in the USA
San Bernardino, CA
21 December 2017